Legacy of One Left Behind

Rachel Hatton

ISBN: 978-1-80128-334-2

Dedication

This book is dedicated to my mother, Margaret Hoey, and my father, William Hoey. The legacy they created throughout their lives has shaped me to be exactly who I am.

I have always felt loved, respected, and valued. You have taught me to be generous, caring, and kind. I will forever be grateful that I was blessed to have you as my parents.

Acknowledgements

This book was written for my children, James, Jessica, and Joseph Hatton. When you remember me, know that my love and care for you three has always been my most important purpose. Thank You, God.

This book was also written to honor so many people we lost on 9/11, including Teddy, Phil, Tim H., Todd, Nester, Tim S. Vinnie, Chris, Billy, Nigel, Mike, Atsushi, Andy, John, Joey. Tim G, Mike M., and so many, many, more. I honor you all. Your legacy lives on.

I want to say thank you to Simon, from Talented Ghost Writers, who helped me make sense of my words and thoughts. I was writing a book for my kids. You said it was for the world. Thank you for helping me honor so many people. Thank you!

A special acknowledgment to Clare George, who pushed me for the last two years to follow my dreams and write this book. You made me pick up the pen.

Thank you, Ben Rees Evans, for helping me create such a wonderful book title.

And lastly, Danny Lavecchia and Mike Capra. We knew them all, we miss them greatly, and we will sit together today honoring each one of them. It's a blessing to have you to share the memories.

About the Author

I reside in Fort Myers, Florida, where I have been compiling these stories to bring you my book Legacy of One Left Behind. I am a proud mother of three awesome children, James, Jessica, and Joseph Hatton. I am a sister of three amazing women and the daughter of an understanding mother.

I work as a foreign exchange options broker for BGC Partners, an affiliate of Cantor Fitzgerald. To feel rewarded, I do different kinds of charity work, from breast cancer awareness to feeding the homeless. I am living a purposeful and meaningful life filled with kindness and gratitude. I am a certified life coach and will pursue that as a career one day.

Losing so many of my closest friends on 9/11 and hoping to honor them really inspired me to write this book. Knowing my children will have this as a legacy book when I am gone inspired me to finish it.

I like tennis, pickleball, and sitting on the beach with a good book when I have downtime. Traveling and seeing how all people in the world live is my true passion.

Preface

James and Jessica Hatton are taken out of class on Sept 11th, 2001. They are told to hurry along with the other children to an assembly at the Catholic school they are attending in London, England. The children, who are eight and seven years old, sit and stare as a television announcer explains on the TV there has been an attack! Two planes hit the towers. They hear the man say and wonder for a minute, can they be the same towers they spent so much time visiting their mother at work? Then they hear a plane has hit the Pentagon in Washington D.C, and another was taken down in Pennsylvania. As the other students sit and their jaws drop at what comes on the screen next, James and Jess look up at their Dad, waiting at the door to take them home. With tears streaming down their faces, the children get up and walk toward their father and away from the screen behind them, showing the towers crashing to the ground.

They ask, *where is mommy?*

Contents

Page Left Blank Intentionally

Chapter 1 – The Beginning

Have you ever met someone who made an important impact on your life? Whether a family member, a friend, or a well-known figure? In your life or the universe, what legacy did the individual leave? What was it about him or her that made him or her so special to you? How long after they were not in your life did you find yourself thinking about the time that you were with that person. How long after they were gone were you still thinking about them in some way, even after time passed on? Were they taken away suddenly, or did they have time to say goodbye?

How would you like to be remembered after your physical life is over? What do you want people to remember about you? What kind of long-term effect do you want to have on the planet, whether through your work, achievements, relationships, or something else? Rachel, like everybody else on the flight to New York, didn't think that anything serious and life-changing would take place when the plane was taking off. She was just toward the end of the movie '*Bridget Jones Diary*.' The flight had been pretty smooth and 30 minutes from landing at the Newark airport. She was waiting patiently, excited to reunite and party with her co-workers, who she hadn't seen in a month.

However, sometimes, life doesn't always go as planned.

A few moments later, Rachel noticed two airline flight attendants standing in the middle of the aisle, almost in a formation. Tears were streaming down their faces. The scene playing out in front of her eyes seemed something out of a movie, just before something big is about to happen – like a plane crash. Rachel couldn't focus on the movie, which automatically shut off after a few minutes. She just kept looking at what was slowly unraveling on the plane. Everyone on the plane was waiting and hoping for the voice of the pilot to come across the PA system, to speak to them and say words of comfort and encouragement. Everyone had woken up one by one. Seats were adjusted. All passengers were sitting silently. What was only five minutes felt like an hour delay to hear the pilot speak. All eyes were on the two women crying silently in the aisle. Many passengers were praying that everything would be alright … the pilot's voice would sound any minute and say, *"Everything is alright."*

No one expected the words that came from the pilot.

"Good morning, ladies and gentlemen ... This is your captain speaking ... I have some news to share ... I need everyone to hear this and follow instructions."

Hearing the captain's calm voice didn't do anything to alleviate the panic that had suddenly erupted in Rachel's chest. She knew in her heart the plane must be about to crash… maybe these were the captain's last words, encouraging strength and bravery in the face of a disaster. At that very moment, she thought about a million things at once and heard very little. All she was thinking about was her kids. Will her kids be okay without her?

"Please watch over my children." At that point in time, just like everybody else on the plane, she was gearing herself for the worst. She expected to die on the plane. She wasn't ready to die, yet she felt a sense of calmness. She just kept thinking about her kids. Are they going to be okay? What will they do without her? Who will make sure they have what they need?

More thoughts came flying. What has she done in her life? Has she been a good person, a good daughter, a good wife, and a sister? Has she done her part to make a difference in the world, so God would let her in heaven? What impact has she left on the world and the people? She was thinking of everything at once … and the best memories of everybody in a flash of light. She thought of her three sisters, whom she had become best friends with after they all became moms, and hoped they would be okay, and her parents, who made her laugh till she cried so many times. In front of her eyes, she saw her loving husband bravely breaking the news to three children that their mother was gone. She was already missing them all greatly. Besides being a loving mother and a good person, she is also a woman who wants to leave something important behind. Every memory from her past flashed through her head and she asked herself, *"How will I be remembered!?"*

The PA system blared to life. Rachel had never expected to hear what the pilot said next…

***

It was a gorgeous morning the day Rachel had boarded an American Airlines flight from London heading to New York City. It was an unusually nice day in London and an equally gorgeous day in New York City. The sky was littered with white fluffy clouds, with the sunlight peeking out every now and then. No one could have fathomed what the day would bring … what a catastrophic event would befall very soon. Rachel certainly didn't think anything bad would happen when she had boarded the plane that fine morning in London. She didn't have a clue, just like the other people who woke up that morning, had breakfast like every other morning, and listened to the radio in the car while going to work or dropping their kids off at school. It was the beginning of September – 9/11/2001. Like Rachel, everyone else had no idea what the day would bring … how the world would be turned upside down in just a matter of a few hours.

Rachel worked for Cantor Fitzgerald, the firm that occupied the top four floors of the World Trade Centers. On the morning of 9/11 , the CEO of Cantor, Howard Lutnick, was taking his son, Kyle, to Kindergarten. It was the first day of school for many people across the U.S.A., a pretty big deal for little kids and their parents alike. It was the perfect day – brisk back-to-school kind of weather when it's not summer anymore. Rachel could feel it – the change in the weather – when she left her house and walked to the car.

She took many deep breaths and tasted the chill in the air, embedding deep within her lungs, but also soothing at the same time. It was the classic September morning, birds were chirping, and everything was calm. The morning air was cool and refreshing as Rachel embarked on the plane and sat at her designated seat. A stewardess walked by, rolling her trolley, and offered snacks. All the passengers sat back and relaxed as the plane took off from the tarmac. It was a five-and-a-half-hour to six-hour journey from London to New York. She decided to watch a movie Bridget Jones Diary, unaware that the first plane had hit the North Tower of the World Trade Center.

Who could have guessed what happened next?

"Passengers, please put your seats in the upright position and the tray tables away."

All the lights on the plane came on as people started to question and wonder aloud what was happening. The TVs had turned off automatically, and although Rachel was annoyed that the TV was shut off, she knew she had to listen to what the pilot was saying, as it seemed serious by the look of the crying stewardesses and the light abruptly coming on.

"Two planes have just hit the World Trade Center in New York City. It's suspected to be a terrorist attack. Please remain calm and do NOT panic. We are going to divert the plane to Halifax, Canada, for safety."

The news hit Rachel like tons of bricks. She jumped out of her seat and started yelling in an instant, *"Please tell me what happened?"* not truly believing what she just heard could be true and thinking so many thoughts swirling in her head. She thought about her team, sitting there at that moment, on the 105th floor of the World Trade Center. The office is made of glass and steel, essentially a gilded cage. The windows are sky-high, as she recalls seeing planes flying outside the ceiling to floor windows. She has seen helicopters go by, and the errant thought flies in her mind, *"If one of those ever hits us, we will never get out."*

She had so many friends in there, some of them for 15 years or more. She unbuckled the seat restraint and got up, continuing to demand answers and clarity.

"Ma'am, please sit down."

"I'm sorry ... I want to know what's going on. There's been an attack? On the World Trade Center?"

"Ma'am, we do not know much at the moment. But... two planes hit the towers in a suspected terrorist attack."

"How bad is it?"

"Ma'am, I cannot tell you. Please cooperate with us... we want to make this journey as safe as possible, given the circumstances."

What the stewardess didn't tell Rachel was that the crew had no idea if their plane was also hijacked or not. Only time would tell if they landed in Halifax. She implored Rachel to sit back down, buckle up, brace for the rest of the journey, and pray that all would be well.

As she was leaving, Rachel asked in a very loud voice, enough for the other passengers to hear the conversation. *"At least tell me what is going on. I have to know what is happening. My... co-workers are in that building right now."*

She looked at Rachel and said, *"You don't want to know, trust me."*

"Try me."

"There are no more World Trade Towers... both crashed to the ground."

Rachel fell to her knees on the plane, wide eyes and hands shaking, the stewardess calmly helping her to her seat. She just knew in her heart from the many years spent in the building that there's no way anyone could have survived.

The plane landed in Halifax, Canada, and the people got out. Everyone was dazed and confused. They didn't know where to go, what to believe, or what was going on. The authorities mandated that everyone should leave their luggage and purses behind on the plane. Just the passengers were instructed to leave.

Rachel, somehow, found a payphone and called her husband, who was still in London at that time.

"Hi... Joe, it's me."

"Oh my God, Rachel! Are you okay? I was so worried... where are you now?"

"NO, I am not. I can't believe this is happening. The plane landed in Halifax... I am in Canada right now. But please... tell me what is happening?"

"I am so sorry, it's bad... the towers collapsed. I was so worried that you would be on your way to the office... oh, thank God."

"Please... give me one name... just one name of one person that you know who survived. I need a name."

The man on the other end of the phone just cried, *"I can't... there isn't one... I am so sorry."*

Rachel knew at that point that she had probably, most definitely, lost all her co-workers in the attack. Meanwhile, she and almost a thousand other people were taken to a motocross raceway in Halifax, Canada. The Red Cross came in on the scene in an instant. They were amazing. They brought in 1000 air mattresses that were blown up immediately. They brought in blankets and a lot of televisions, set up food stations, and then went person to person, asking if they needed any medication and other help.

They were absolute lifesaving heroes for the passengers who were still shell-shocked. The next day, something even more amazing happened. The residents of Halifax visited the motocross raceway and asked five or ten stranded people at a time to come home with them. There, the people would shower and try to come back to normalcy. The acts of kindness never stopped, even more so in times of great calamity. Rachel couldn't believe how complete strangers took her home and gave her fresh clothes to wear after she showered. They gave her their cell phone, so she could remain in touch with people back home. The people never stopped coming every day. Different people came in every day, with more food and clothes, offering an ear to listen to devastated people cry if that's what they needed. Anything you needed; they were there to help. And they wanted nothing in return. They just wanted to help.

Freshly showered, Rachel sat in front of the TV, watching the news, and waiting for any word that someone she knew may have been found. But none came, so she just sat and cried. One resident, while making her daily rounds among the stranded passengers, saw her crying. With a plate of freshly made food in her hand, she walked over to Rachel and just sat there, next to the crying woman.

At that time, she felt the loneliest. She also thought a lot about her life. She shouldn't have been alive, yet she was.

"Why me? Why did I not make it to New York, walk into the building, go off the elevator, and sit there with my co-workers? Why did they leave me here? What am I doing here? I don't know my purpose."

She stayed in Halifax for several days, and that stay was such a painful time in her life. She thought about many things during this time. The reflection brought out deep feelings of a purpose of figuring out what her purpose is on this earth and in this life.

From that day onward, her life changed forever. She became a different parent, a different wife, a better friend, and a different daughter. She became kinder, more generous, and a more caring person. She never took a day for granted again.

"The purpose of life is a life of purpose." ***-Robin Sharma***

If you have a loving family, a great job, and supportive friends, you may be wondering why sometimes it doesn't feel like enough or that something is missing. It can feel like you're walking numbly through life – or like you're rudderless, floating aimlessly without intent or direction – when you lack purpose and sense. On the other hand, finding purpose and meaning can connect you to something bigger, giving you ambition, intention, enthusiasm, and energy. The good news is that it's never too late to discover your intent if you don't know what it is. Here are five suggestions to help you discover your life's meaning and intent.

1. Read

Reading is one of the simplest and most open ways to find meaning in your life because meaning and intent are closely linked to the concept of connection. Reading is fundamentally about making connections. Reading the words of people we'll never meet brings us closer to them. It transports us to various eras and locations, many of which are foreign to us. According to studies, people who read the Bible or other religious texts have a stronger sense of intent than those who don't, but this isn't only due to the religious element. According to studies, people who read secular works such as fiction and poetry have a greater sense of meaning. Consider some of history's most popular literary characters. From *To Kill a Mockingbird's* Atticus Finch battling for social justice to The Lord of the Rings' Frodo Baggins journeying to Mordor, so many characters share an unshakeable sense of intent. The more we see purpose in other people's lives – fictional or real – the more likely we are to see it in our own.

Reading has been credited by some of the world's most inspiring and motivated people with giving them purpose, so if you feel like your life lacks significance, something as easy as picking up a book will help you separate what matters about your life.

2. Fight for Something Worthwhile

When it comes to inequality, most of us can identify certain reasons that are more bothersome than others. Maybe it's brutality against children or people who have to endure war and famine. It may be a matter of racism or sexism. It may be animal rights, health, or sustainability and conservation concerns. Your own or loved ones' experiences may have led you to be passionate about such topics, such as assisting people with addiction or mental health issues. Most of us have causes that we are passionate about. Fighting for something greater than ourselves can be a very fulfilling way to find meaning and purpose. Consider what irritates and angers you the most, and then consider how you can assist in resolving the issue. Thousands of organizations and causes are in dire need of assistance – and sometimes, by working for what you believe is the common good, you will discover new ways to make a difference that are genuinely unique to you. Finding a way to repurpose your talent, passion, and expertise to bring about social change can be much more beneficial than donating your time and money to support others. You can write articles to raise awareness about a topic you care about if you're a good writer.

If you enjoy public speaking, you can use your expertise to educate people or visit schools to talk to children about issues that are important to you after the pandemic. If you enjoy music, you can learn how it can be used for therapy. Perhaps you can seek a career change in which you can align your talents with a meaningful cause.

If you're not sure what your cause is or how you can improve, try asking yourself the following questions:

- What is your favorite pastime?
- What is something that comes naturally to you?
- What is it that you are passionate about?
- What would you do if you could change one thing in the world?

3. Be among People Who Encourage You

It's also beneficial to take a moment to consider the people you hang out with. Limit time spent with those you feel an obligation to see and spend time with and make more time for those whom you do want to spend your time with. It's easy to feel depressed when negative people surround you, and it's much harder to feel motivated when these people aren't involved in making meaningful changes. Of course, you don't have to cut these people from your life to find meaning and intent. However, it is beneficial to spend time with people who inspire and motivate you to make a difference. Although reading about inspirational people can be beneficial, it can also be daunting. Suppose you read about a civil rights activist who awakened a generation. In that case, you might feel inspired in a certain respect, but you might also feel daunted as if no matter how hard you try, you'll never be able to make such a difference. However, small actions can have a big effect, so if you have people in your life who inspire and encourage you, try to spend more time with them. Consider accompanying a friend to the next social justice talk or rally if you have one. If you have a friend who volunteers at a soup kitchen in your area, see if you can join them.

4. Pay Attention to What Others Are Doing

Many of us are the harshest critics of ourselves. We are quick to notice things like creativity, enthusiasm, and intellect in others, but we are less quick to notice these qualities in ourselves. Asking others for their suggestions and opinions – what they like about you, what they think you're good at, what makes you unique – can be extremely helpful. When you hear and consider what other people like about you, it will provide you with insight into your beliefs and abilities, which can help you pursue a meaningful life.

Suppose anyone tells you that you are exceptionally empathic or that they find it easy to open up to you. In that case, you might realize that you can use this trait to support others by retraining as a counselor or working on helplines. It's important to remember that it's never too late to change careers. Suppose anyone tells you that you're caring, patient, or willing to relate with teens in a way that others can't. In that case, it can strengthen some of the ideals and passions that you already have but haven't completely realized. The reality is that recognizing what you care about most of what you're inherently good at can be oddly challenging, simply because they're so embedded in us that we don't recognize them. Solicit advice and suggestions from those around you, and then pay attention to what they have to say. Finally, don't forget to pay attention to yourself. What does your intuition tell you when you think about a cause or a passion? Do you really want to volunteer for a specific charity, or are you just doing it because it's the right thing to do? Do you really want to try that new hobby, or are you just doing it because you don't know what else to do? Don't do something just for the sake of doing it, and don't do something that makes you unhappy. It will feel right when you find your reason. So trust your instincts because you are the only one who knows what is best for you.

5. Assist Others

It's commonly acknowledged that some feelings and behaviors that promote our well-being significantly impact our sense of intent, with kindness and selflessness being two of them. Volunteering, assisting others, and finding a way to give back are all linked to a more positive and purposeful life.

There are many avenues in which you can assist others. You can donate money to a cause you care for, volunteer your time for a charity, or personally assist people in your community – for example, visiting an elderly neighbor to keep them company or offering to do the shopping for a sick friend. Suppose you want to support others every day or once a week. In that case, the simple act of being compassionate and helping others will go a long way toward making you feel like your life has meaning. It's also worth noting that once you start helping others, you'll most likely meet new people who will inspire you even more. Volunteering once a week at a homeless shelter, for example, will introduce you to people who devote their lives to helping others who are less fortunate than themselves. It is sometimes these encounters that have the greatest impact on us. Finding reason and meaning in our lives does not normally happen easily, no matter how hard we look. Finding our true intent can take months, years, or even a lifetime, but some argue that the quest is the most important of all. It's possible that what motivates and inspires you will change over time. This is just a natural part of our development as people. It does not imply that we are giving up on something.

It doesn't matter what act, hobby, or work you find that gives you purpose; all that matters is that you get something out of it. Take the time to focus on your current interest or cause as you go along if you decide to try it. Ask yourself if the new path you're on feels like the right one for you; and if it doesn't, it's fine to change directions.

Chapter 2 – Life Before

Have you ever considered what your life's goal is? Some of us spend our entire lives trying to find out what we're here for. Some people struggle, and others excel. Then there are others who are aware of their intent but are still distracted from it. People who know their life's purpose tend to live more fulfilling lives than people who don't. Since you know who you are, where you came from, and where you're going, you tend to live each day to the fullest. Here are a few pointers that will help you see where you stand in your life.

Knowing the meaning behind your life makes it easier to concentrate on the things that are most important to you. You will find your course and stay away from distractions if you keep your attention on one specific target. When you know what you want, it will assist you in discovering your true passion, which will serve as a powerful motivator for you to accomplish something exceptional. Whether it's a childhood dream or a new way of life, your ambition will drive you to achieve your objectives.

People who know what they want to do with their lives are unstoppable. They live their lives in accordance with their mission. People who are unsure of their life's meaning are unsure of what they want and therefore they spend their time on unfulfilling pursuits. When you have a life goal, you articulate it often and center your decisions, emotions, feelings, and actions around it. An individual who understands their intent is more likely to have a positive impact in their work, which leads to a sense of fulfillment. Values are an important part of a person's life. They go hand in hand with meaning. Values are the principles that direct our life choices and help us identify our objectives. They're what tell us whether or not we're on the right track. They're what help us find and communicate with those who share our worldview. Knowing your life's meaning allows you to live with dignity. People who understand their life's meaning are aware of who they are, what they do, and why they do it. It's much easier to live a life that's true to your core values when you know yourself. People who are clear about their reason note an uptick in synchronicity and serendipity in their lives. As a result of this, they have a greater sense of confidence and faith in other people, and they consider themselves to be a part of the universe. People who live their lives with a purpose also report that they are often living with grace. "Until one is committed, there is hesitancy, the chance to withdraw, often ineffectiveness," says German poet Johann Wolfgang von Goethe. Amazing things will happen when you commit to living your life with a purpose. People who have discovered their calling appear to exist in the universal stream of consciousness. Rather than battling it, they encourage things to happen and change in their lives. They are more likely to test themselves and face their fears. People who know their life's meaning love every moment of it. They enjoy living a purpose-driven life and are better at approaching any situation in a creative manner. When you're inspired by a higher cause, even the most mundane task becomes beautiful and imaginative.

The advantages of living a life with meaning are obvious. When you have a sense of intent in life, you begin to live positively and search out new opportunities. You begin to do something that you believe can make a difference. When you live life with meaning, it has a positive impact on your relationships. You seek out new relationships, nurture the ones you already have, and strengthen your bonds with those around you. You become a role model for your family and friends by being more helpful to the people you care about. You appear to be more curious about life and strive to avoid destructive behaviors in favor of positive ones that will help you make a difference in the world. So, if you're really searching for your life's reason, don't wait any longer. Make it a priority, and you can soon experience the peace and serenity that comes with living a life with a purpose. But for us to find our purpose, we need to start from the beginning. We need to go back from where everything started - when we were little, and the experiences we gathered designed our thinking for the later years. Rachel's beginnings were humble. The family was poor but still managed to make ends meet, somehow.

Her father, Billy, was funny, good-looking, and personable. But he was a heavy drinker. He drank most days, which may have made it hard for him to hold down a good job. Instead, he held a lot of jobs to make ends meet. He dug graves and bartended at a local pub. He was also a longshore man – a laborer at the docks. He was once enlisted in the Merchant Marines as well. He did what he could to put food on the table. Her mother, Peggy, was much younger than her dad. Twelve years younger, in fact. She endured a tougher life than most and took care of herself from a very young age. This pretty, young woman found a sense of comfort, love, and security when she became a life partner with this man who she loved deeply. She also wanted to help the family with the financial struggles, so she waitressed.

However, there were times when it was difficult to manage the finances of the household, which is why they also took government assistance. Both worked to get by and provide what they could for the girls. They didn't have much, that was for sure. When the girls were kids, they lived in several different houses. Sometimes, a kind friend lent his or her couch for a few nights. It was like an adventure, yet sometimes, they felt like a huge burden on other families, being at their houses and eating their food. But that's just how it was. The girls always made the best of their situation. They had lots of good times in their house as well. They shared a set of bunkbeds in a bedroom and would jump from one to the other, laughing their heads off until either someone got hurt or dad yelled, "I am coming up there with the belt." He didn't really use it, but for some reason, Rachel was petrified he really would. It was a child's fear. Her parents loved each other and their girls.

They tried to create a space as often as possible that felt like a home for the family. Rachel loved the times when the whole family was together, either during a bad storm or just a rainy Sunday, and they would marathon a movie series. She loved the warm feeling of everyone being together. They knew how to make each other laugh. Sometimes they would just be sitting around, and out of nowhere, Rachel's mother would tell a joke or a story, and before she even finished, one person would start laughing and then another, and they would all laugh until they cried, especially when telling a funny story. The family was Irish Catholic, which meant that each girl had First Communion Party. Rachel had hers in second grade, which lasted for three days. The entire extended family attended. It was such an important celebratory occasion. There was plenty of alcohol and food, and everyone partied until late into the night. The uncles and aunts left their kids behind after the festivities ended. They would come back for them the next day but once again start drinking, so the kids would stay again.

Rachel's mom thought this was hilarious, and she would do her best to throw together all that they had to feed everyone. Rachel's dad was a gentleman who always looked his best. His perfectly ironed pants and not a hair out of place ever would never elude you to the fact that he most likely didn't have a dime in his pocket. Everywhere he went, people wanted to shake his hand. He would refer to a lot of people as *"My man"* because he could never remember anyone's name. To him, everyone was just - my man!

Rachel loved going to the bar with her dad even as a little girl. She would sit up at the bar with a coke and a bag of chips and watch all the people drinking and singing, and she loved it. She and her sisters would play the shuffleboard game in the bar, and everyone would hand them change to play and get snacks.

She was also very close to her cousin, Jackie, who lived in the suburbs. Jackie did not live like Rachel and her family. No, she lived in a big house with a white picket fence and a lot of grass. Rachel would go stay with her whenever she was allowed and begged for Jackie to stay with her. They called each other country mouse and city mouse. Rachel thought Jackie's family was rich, and it really had inspired her from a very young age to want to work and get money because she knew she wanted a white picket fence around her house, too, when she grew up. When Rachel visited Jackie, they would ride bikes and play in Jackie's human-sized dollhouse in her backyard. She had MTV on her television and didn't have to get up to change the channel. Rachel loved going there. When Jackie would visit Rachel, they would knock on doors and sweep the pavements of Rachel's neighbors for 25 or 50 cents. Once they gathered enough money, they would go to the corner store, buy a pickle, roll, and potato chips, and make a sandwich with the pickle and chips. They loved it. Their visits and experiences at each other's homes were very different, and they loved to learn from each other. Rachel also found happiness and comfort when she was with her sisters. Nicki would let her come with her and hang out as they were closest in age. They would just hang out on street corners or find an abandoned house and make a fort as though they now owned the property. Sometimes they would go to the public pool and go swimming. Nicki was very competitive and would always get in the swimming competitions at the pool. Rachel was not so athletic and would be in awe of how fierce she was and how she was never afraid to go up against anyone.

Rachel found safety and comfort with her sister, Tracy, who was a second mother to her. Rachel would climb in the bed whenever she had a night terror, or there was fighting in the house, and Tracy would hold her hand until she fell asleep, assuring her everything would be okay. She would make sure Rachel looked her best for whatever event was happening. When she had picture day at school or went somewhere, Tracy would help her find something to wear and make sure her hair looked nice. Tracy would always make sure Rachel had whatever she needed. When Rachel was bullied on her way home from school, Tracy and Nicki would step in and make sure the bully knew who her sisters were. Nancy was four years younger than Rachel, so she treated her just like the rest of her dolls. She wanted to play with her, position her, fix her beautiful strawberry blonde hair, and then fix it again. Nancy was a good sport and was always happy to play along. Rachel loved her little sister.

As a child, Rachel didn't realize how poor the family was, probably because her parents raised their four daughters in an environment where everyone was poor. Their neighbors were poor, so Rachel didn't really know what she was missing. She didn't know that they didn't have the finer things in life because she wasn't exposed to "those things." Rachel spent most days with her very best friend, Vicki. They would play games like kick the can, different card games, or jacks. They would recruit other kids in the neighborhood to play dodgeball, catch and kiss, or a friendly game of tag. You didn't need to have a lot of money, or sometimes any, to play most of these games. Rachel and Vicki would be creative in making up fun games to play. Some mornings while getting ready for school, Rachel would see a homeless man sitting at the kitchen table, with holes in his shoes and wearing an old coat that was three times his size. The patriarch of the family used to serve breakfast to the homeless, who found their way to his table, before himself or his family. That was just his way. From a very young age, Rachel's father had taught her the value of giving what you can to people who don't have, even though they have nothing to give you back. Rachel had no choice but to believe in Santa because somehow, every Christmas, there would be lots of presents under the tree, no matter what. Later in life, Rachel often wondered where her parents got the presents from because she knew they couldn't afford them. The family went through hardships wrought by financial difficulties, but they got by.

Rachel witnessed the love her parents had for each other and the support, and deep down, she wanted the same for herself. She also had something else inside her, and that was determination and drive. She became very ambitious from a very young age. Somewhere around the age of 14, she began to hustle for money. How? There was a woman who drove around the neighborhood in a white van. She would pick up thc kids in thc ncighborhood. Imagine getting into a van with a stranger at the age of 14, having your parents have no idea where you are going, with who, and coming back with money in your pocket. But these were the 80's - different times. There was also a side-hustle. She would hand the kids boxes full of candy and drive them to faraway neighborhoods, from where the kids lived. There, the kids would knock on doors and sell the candy for 50 cents a box. This was a commission-based job, so she would hand over a dime for each box sold. It was lucrative. Sometimes, Rachel would come home with $30 in her pocket. That's how she started working - selling candy door to door. This is how she learned how to make money at a very young age, as well as the value of money. At the age of 16, she went to a hardware supply company and posed as her sister, who didn't want the job, but it was her job interview. No sense to waste a potentially good opportunity, right? She got the job, too, even after she came clean to the interviewers about the intentional mix-up. So, in a lot of ways, it was the circumstances of her upbringing that made her ambitious. Her parents could not give them much, but Rachel took pride in going and getting it for herself. They didn't have any money, but she always knew if she really wanted something, there was a way to attain it. There was always a way to earn money.

Rachel thought if she can make money selling candy door to door, she can take the money and earn more. There was a penny candy store at the street corner in the neighborhood. She would go there and buy 50 cents worth of candy, then sell the product at school for five cents per piece. She made money every way it was possible, every way she could – from the age of 14 and up. She was a born hustler. So, when she was 18 years old, graduating high school, she knew there was only one path for her, and that was going to be to get a job.

Young Rachel went down to the stock exchange, took a test, and started working at the stock exchange. She procured a job that paid $11,000 a year. This is where her career really started. At first, she worked as a runner, and then in the pit, grabbing tickets off people running in and out of the crazy pits. This was something she knew she could excel in. She loved doing this. She loved the people, the crowd, the craziness, and the partying. She absolutely loved it. One day when Rachel was standing in the pit and a man yelled "sold" to another man. She was very curious about this transaction. Is one person going to win and one going to lose on this trade? She had to find out. That was the first question of many she would need and want to ask at the stock exchange, but she felt it was a big scary man's world, though, and she was just an 18-year-old girl, running around through the pits like a crazy maniac. But she loved this feeling she had when she was at work. She loved how she had some semblance of control over her life after the tumultuous childhood she had experienced. It wasn't always sunshine and good times at her home while growing up. There were times when there was incredible uncertainty in her life. Young Rachel often wished she could run away from her life and everything. This lack of control spurred a determination and a fire inside her, and money gave her power. Running through the various pits and attending every happy hour after work, Rachel started to get to know people on the floor of the exchange. One woman, in particular, took a liking to Rachel. Her name was Betse. She was young and nice, but she stood her ground against many screaming men, and she knew exactly what she was doing. Rachel wanted to be just like her. The woman helped young Rachel tremendously. She groomed her after taking the girl under her wing. She taught her everything that she knew about the stock exchange. Rachel was hired for a specific job as her assistant, a specialist clerk, which was the beginning of many jobs she would have on the exchange over the next ten years.

Also, then the men seemed to be betting on everything, even how long the cockroach they had captured on the floor was going to live. They named it and bet thousands on how long it would live. Then they paid an intern to eat it. Everything about being on the exchange was amazing and fun to Rachel. She wanted to learn everything, and people like Betse were more than willing to teach the young, eager girl. She learned many different jobs and did them well. She knew that to succeed in the world, she couldn't let anything get in the way of her advancement and growth. She showed up every day, asking more and more questions, went out to the bars, and met more and more people. She was not old enough to go to the bars, but that didn't stop her. She knew on Thursdays there would be a big gang from the exchange bonding over beers, and she had to be there, so she took her friend's fake ID and sat in the bar. This was life! She was making money, she was making friends, and her life was starting to feel like she was completely in charge of it. *"How successful am I going to be at this job,"* she often thought.The secret to success is hard work, BUT it is also not to let people get in the way, not let them stand in the way, or tell you, you aren't good or smart enough, or you don't know or you can't. You just keep asking questions and more questions until the answers come. And you align yourself with the right people… the ones who don't want to knock you down but help you soar. This is how you WILL achieve all your goals and purposes. Rachel did that. The people she worked with at the stock exchange were the same people who she worked with at Cantor Fitzgerald. So, for her to lose them in 9/11, to lose them to the crash of the World Trade Center, it was a big loss. When the towers collapsed, she lost three of her best friends - Tim, Nigel, and Timmy. They were gone, and she was still here. Why? Was there a reason? What would she do now after her life collapsed and burned, much like the towers had?

A good career, a loving family, and a strong social network may seem to be the perfect formula for a happy life. Those who can check all of those boxes, however, can feel as if something is missing — and that "something" is their life's goal. Finding your intent is more than a cliché or a pipe dream that will never come true. It's a tool for living a richer, happier, and healthier life that far too few people want to use.

What could she do to check all the boxes while remembering and honoring the fallen?

Chapter 3 – Finding Hope

Life isn't without flaws. We all have our problems, and bad things happen to us all the time. Things can go wrong, even though we don't want them to, and they sometimes do to the point that we become frustrated and everything seems to be dark.

It's important that we not only accept this but also acknowledge that we can do something about it. We believe that it is how we react to adversity that defines us, not the circumstances. We'll need the requisite skills to turn things around and make the most of what we've got. It all begins with basic things that you can recall while you are going through a difficult time.

For Rachel, one of the darkest and most difficult days was the ones she spent in Halifax. Those days were devoid of all hope as by then, she had learned how none of her friends had made it out. None had lived. So, what was there, if not hope?

She was still alive, wasn't she? A world of possibilities, choices, and decisions awaited Rachel, but what did she want? She spent days contemplating what had happened, what would happen, and who was gone. She thought about so many different things - about the past, the present, and the future – but mostly, she thought about what she was going to do now. Like most people who survive a fatal accident or a near-death experience, Rachel also questioned the purpose of her existence. Why was she still alive? Why did she even want to be alive? What were her thoughts and feelings? She spent those days in confusion, not knowing which direction to turn to or what path to take. She was in a dark place, just waiting for something or someone to grab her hand and pull her out. It so happened that she was very good friends with a client. His name was Steve, and he lived in New Jersey while working in New York. After several days passed, she called him. Even before getting the words out of her mouth, he informed her about a ferry leaving Halifax and going to Bar Harbor, Maine, which would be a 10-hour drive for him from

New York.

"Get on that ferry, Rachel. I will be there to get you," Steve finished the call.

It was always like this with him. It took him just a minute to jump into hero mode and devise a plan of action to save or help the people he cared about, which was Rachel in this instance. She smiled in relief - the first time in ages. She gathered the few belongings she had gotten together while in Halifax and went to the ferry station. She got on the right ferry, and the next thing she knew, she was sitting in a café with Steve.

They reminisced about all the people in their lives, the same people they both knew from work. They shared stories about a couple of funny guys named Pepe and Nigel, and a guy named Timmy, who was one of Rachel's really close friends. Timmy had recently thrown his wife, Katie, a birthday party at their home, and everyone from work was there. Of course, they were there. They were like one big family.

"All my co-workers from the party died in the towers," Rachel said to Steve. *"It's just so hard to believe we were all together, and now they are all gone!"*

Hours were spent like this, just talking and sharing the stories and crying and laughing. It was a comforting experience to have someone to listen to and talk to. It was a relief to be with someone who knew what Rachel was going through and feeling at that moment. She was lucky to have Steve in her life. He was a good friend who didn't hesitate at all about making the long drive.

A very tearful reunion took place when Rachel met up with her parents and sisters in a diner near Steve's house. He was delivering their daughter safely back to the family. They all thanked him, and Rachel's mom held her very tight. Her parents had been out on a boat on 9/11 and didn't know the magnitude of what was taking place. They also had no idea that Rachel was on her way to New York.

She wanted to surprise her mom and arrive at their home on the weekend. She loved to surprise her parents with gifts or have a special day planned for them. Her parents, Peg and Bill, found out that their daughter was on a plane and now in Halifax and that also their oldest daughter Tracy had been stuck in the air, as the landing gear wasn't working on her plane. Bill immediately began to pray. It was all he could do in this situation.

Rachel spent the next couple of days coming back into the city with her mom and sisters. She attended a gathering at a hotel conference room. So many people were posting pictures of their loved ones they were praying to see once again and yearning for a chance to say goodbye.

Just seeing the pictures of her friends and so many more and knowing the families of those people who were looking for them, not knowing if they were even coming back, was enough to bring Rachel to her knees. She had been lucky. She was alive when these people were grieving, wearing the pain all over them.

Despite the glaring evidence, some people still held hope that they would come back. It was a difficult time - all the more difficult when the wives of her colleagues and really close friends looked at her, and all she could see them thinking is, *"Why is she alive?"* They may not have felt that way, but Rachel heard it in their tears, saw it in their eyes, and believed it in her heart.

"No one wants me to be alive."

It made Rachel think long and hard about life, about the unfairness of everything, and about how she was alive when everybody else was dead and gone. How was it fair? She was going home to her family while the ones who died couldn't return to their families. Did she deserve to be alive? She didn't want to be alive and well on the earth, and she struggled for such a long time to hide the feeling and change the narrative of her thoughts. She hated the expression, *'Everything happens for a reason,'* and questioned, *'Does it?'* Do we just say this to placate our troubled and grieving hearts? How could everything happen for a reason? How could such a thing happen? So many people died on that day. Was there a reason it happened? People, my friends, were just going to work!

She thought day and night. She used to think, *"Why am I here? Please give me a sign. Please tell me what you want me to do. What am I supposed to do? What is life about?"*

The answers started to come little by little. She started to think back to how she was in London, to begin with, and not starting her day in NYC on 9/11. She worked with about 14 men on the FX Options Desk at Cantor Fitzgerald. Over a few days, she heard her boss, Danny, speaking to a few guys about taking a job to go be a boss in the London office.

Rachel thought, *why isn't he asking me*, and decided to go right into his office and find out. *"Excuse me, Danny. Am I chopped liver? I would like to be considered for the London job!"*

Danny was shocked that she had the nerve to walk into his office and he liked that about her, so a couple of days later, he said, *"Pack your bags, Rachel. The job is yours!"*

She and her husband packed up their three little kids, sold her house, and a month later, they moved. Rachel, Timmy, and the whole New York gang were already plotting her return to NYC as soon as she arrived in London. They missed her already. So, a month later, on 9/11, she was heading back to see everyone and work in the New York office. *What if Danny hadn't given me the job in London*, she thought. *What if I flew on Monday, not Tuesday?* She was certain she already knew the answer to these questions, but in her mind, she had to ask them anyway. *Why am I here?*

What if Rachel was placed on the earth to help people who need it? What if her goal and mission were to help people in need? Right now, the company is in need. She remembered Howard Lutnick had lost his brother in the attack, and he was doing everything he could to rebuild here. *He needs help. The families are in need of me to help keep the company going*, she thought to herself.

She went back to London and through herself into her job. She worked 18-20 hours a day, rebuilding the New York office from London because it had crumbled completely. She used to start her day from 6:30 a.m. until 11 p.m., tirelessly and diligently.

She used to work and work and felt her life didn't have any semblance of control. It felt out of control, once again. She felt that she had no control over anything in her life. Each day was the same. She would leave for work at 6:30 a.m. in the morning and come home at 11 p.m. every night, hating the life she was living. She felt like a zombie going through the motions of a day with nothing inside her. It was so empty. She was grieving.

She felt like the inner child in her was back, with full force, and everything swirled in a mass of chaos and confusion. She didn't have any control again. She was burnt out beyond belief and barely functioning. She was like the juggler who tried hard to keep all the balls in the air and make everything work, despite everything going wrong. She felt that her life had no purpose. This went on for a long period of time.

Sometimes, God does for us what we can't do for ourselves and steps in. Rachel was not enjoying her children. She was so exhausted on the weekend. She wanted to be the mother they knew. She wanted to be happy and fun. The darkness she felt kept telling her she did not deserve to be happy. She did not deserve these amazing children. Too many others were still suffering. She was in pain. She was an empty shell, not seeking help, not speaking to anyone, and not seeing friends. She was just getting by. The one thing she was doing well was pouring everything she had into work and making sure the New York office would be running and profiting again.

She would work tirelessly many late nights with a crew of diligent and loyal-to-the-cause co-workers right by her side. Cappy and Richard gave up their nights to be there. Neil, Craig Paul, Wayne, and Laurie all were there to lend a hand whenever they were needed, and the team that was having breakfast at the desk in the morning found themselves ordering a late dinner to get ready for a long night ahead.

Rachel hired Billy Clarke to begin to rebuild the NYC team. Billy would leave his family in NY and stay in London to help rebuild BGC New York. They worked late into the night. Everyone was exhausted. Day after day, night after night, she was always there.

People in the market took notice of the work she was doing in a crisis and under a great deal of stress, and they were greatly impressed. Soon after, the offers from her competitors started pouring in. They offered her opportunities to go back to New York. That had been a fear to go back to New York with Cantor because she knew she would expect to see her co-workers, and they were gone. They also offered her money and lots of it.

She called her dad, *"Dad, I have been offered a job to go back to NY and a million dollars!"*

"OMG, honey. You're like a baseball player," her father replied.

She didn't care as much about the money as she did hearing her father so proud. She thought about it. New York housed her family and her old friends. She knew she could not put 9/11 behind her. It was forever a part of her. But for a minute, she thought, *"Maybe I can move forward."* She had been stuck in anger, sadness, and guilt and knew the best thing for her to do was start fresh.

So, she did it… She walked out of the firm. She flew to New York, where her family waited. She was ordered to stay out of the market for ten months. It was called a non-compete. That is God doing for you what you can't do for yourself because Rachel was on the verge of a breakdown. The ten months sitting out was the therapy she needed to get her head straight. What did she do during this time? She spent this time focusing on her children, who were very young. She became the mom she always wanted to be, taking her youngest, Jojo, to storybook time, and playing games with James and Jess often. She was present in their lives. She tried meditation and to focus on what she needed from the inside, to find out who she was and what the universe was, and what who she called God wanted her to do.

*"The opportunity to step away from everything and take a break is something that shouldn't be squandered." **-Harper Reed***

Life rushes at a breakneck speed, and we're always tempted to keep up. Days fly by, and we strive to cram so much into them and get so much done and to such particular goals that when we don't, when we "fall short" of our goals, we feel as if we're drowning.

At least, that was what Rachel had been feeling for the longest time.

When you establish objectives and take action to accomplish big things in life, it's tempting to push things too far and expect yourself to go, go, go all the time, like a machine, and produce results.

However, we are not robots. Even with things we enjoy, we aren't supposed to go 24 hours a day and seven days a week. We must learn to take a step back. We must be disciplined in separating our constant "productivity" from the rest of our lives. There's an inverse link between the number of hours you work in a week and your actual production — and if that's the case, the same might be said for the amount of time you spend working continuously throughout the day. It wears you down when you're slaving away at your desk, never leaving, and ticking off that prison of a to-do list. No matter how hard you work, it seems like there are always more things to do, and you're never good enough, fast enough, or efficient enough, and then the day is over.

When inner chaos begins to blossom, it's time to stop what you're doing, take a step back, and do something else. What exactly does that imply? Everyone's situation is unique. Going outside, spending time with family or friends, exercising, playing an instrument, watching a show, listening to music, taking a walk, petting a cat, and who knows what else! Whatever it is, it is a break from the turmoil of to-do lists, objectives, expectations, and self-criticism. It's a reminder that you're here, right now, and in command — not your to-do list, tasks, or laptop. YOU'RE THE ONE.

There's a lot to be said for taking a step back and taking some time off. Not only does it help us re-energize our creativity, but it also helps us do more — in a sense, stepping away from our work every now and then, rather than focusing on it for long periods of time – and helps us get more done better.

*"Taking a break can lead to breakthroughs." **-Russell Eric Donda***

So, if you're feeling overwhelmed today, take a step back. Your job will be there for you when you return, you'll be refreshed, and you'll be more in touch with your best self, which is where your best work is done. Do you want to do more? Do you want to live a happier and healthier life? Do you want to be more inventive in your day-to-day tasks? Do you want to keep your sanity? Take a breather and choose to be present in the moment, whatever that may be. To take a "step back," all you have to do is give yourself some time and patience. Wait for the dust to settle before making a decision or going on, rather than reacting rashly.

A "step back" allows you to calm down when you're experiencing strong emotions. Our "emotional brains" react faster than our "thinking brains" regularly. When we experience strong emotions, it can be difficult to think clearly at the moment, and this is when our emotions might take precedence over our better judgment.

The worst of all, the hot/cold empathy gap demonstrates that we are often unable to foresee how we would react in a highly charged emotional scenario until we have a first-hand experience with it. We all have a "Jekyll and Hyde" dual personality inside us, and who emerges depends a lot on our emotional state. When you're dealing with strong emotions, taking a "step back" is frequently the only way to calm down and come to your senses. A "step back" in this scenario could be stepping into another room, taking a brief stroll, sleeping on a problem, or simply reminding yourself to take ten deep breaths. You can redirect your present journey by taking a "step back."

You may need to take a literal step back to correct yourself if you are wandering through nature and find yourself on the wrong route. While taking this "step back" and admitting you made a mistake may be annoying or uncomfortable, it is surely preferable to continue down the wrong path. Is that correct?

Taking a metaphorical "step back" can help us redirect our life paths, whether it's in our profession, relationship, health, habit, or personal ambition.

The ability to take a "step back" provides us with freedom. It implies that our current life choices do not bind us and that we have the ability to examine and change them. When your beliefs and interests are no longer served by a relationship, a career, or even ambitions, it may be necessary to take a vacation from them. Instead of blindly pushing forward, we should take a "step back" and consider how our life choices are working out in the long run and if we should continue with them or not.

A "step back" helps you to relax and take in the scenery. Our ability to "take a step back" is also crucial to our pleasure and well-being.

It might be tough to find time to relax and be grateful for what you currently have when you are continuously pushing forward and searching for the next item you want. Sometimes, all you need do is take a breather and take in the scenery. Take a moment to sit down and think about all the nice things that have happened in your life. Consider pleasant memories. Make a list of things for which you are grateful. Consider meditating. Appreciate natural phenomena on a daily basis. Take part in activities that will knock you off your feet and leave you speechless (like watching a beautiful sunset or gazing at the stars). When we aren't paying attention to what is directly in front of us, life slips us by rapidly. Taking a "step back" allows us to unwind and enjoy the present moment. We must all strike a good balance between “moving forward” and “taking a step back” in our lives. While it's vital to push ourselves and be ambitious, it's also critical that we take time to relax and enjoy ourselves. Make time in your life for both.

Chapter 4 – Purpose

*"The person without a purpose is like a ship without the rudder." –**Thomas Carlyle***

What is the meaning of the word 'purpose'? What does it mean to have a purpose in life? If you look up the meaning of this word in the dictionary, you'll find a few definitions.

When used as a noun:

The reason for which something is done or created or something exists.

A person's sense of resolve or determination.

A particular requirement or consideration, typically one that is temporary or restricted in scope or extent.

When used as a verb:

Have as one's intention or objective.

A million and one questions must be swirling in your mind after reading different definitions. Have you ever thought about this… are you the reason something exists? Do you have determination? What are your intentions for seeking a life of quality and what are you willing to do to achieve that?

You may be a parent; therefore, you are most certainly the reason something exists. How do you interact with your children? Do you feel determined to be the best parent to the offspring you have chosen to bring into this world? We all came into this world with a purpose, and your kind and nurturing parenting may most certainly have a great impact on helping your child one day find their purpose.

Many people are unaware that discovering one's purpose is a lifelong endeavor. It's true how only a select handful is fortunate enough to discover their calling early in life. Life's lottery winners usually go about their business with relative ease.

However, the likelihood is that you are not one of the fortunate few. You're probably more like me than you think. You've struggled to figure out what you were sent for on this earth to do time and time again. Your search has largely been based on trial and error. There's no reason to be concerned if this describes you. There are two main causes behind this.

- Some people live their entire lives without ever completely understanding what their life's purpose is. They never find out because they never look for it. And since they never seek, the majority of their days are spent haphazardly, with little substance and a constant sense of emptiness. That isn't you, though.
- You are most likely like the majority of individuals. You've discovered your calling, or at least you thought you had, only to discover a few years later that it wasn't actually your *true* calling after all. And that's fine since our life's mission isn't a one-time event.

The Reality of Finding Your Life's Purpose

The truth is that your life's purpose is complex. When you first start looking for your purpose, you take the first one you come across (that first exterior layer), only to grow out of it. Then you go on to the following level's goal. And for a time, you'll be living on purpose again, albeit one that differs from what you believed it was only a few years ago, but you'll eventually outgrow your current purpose and discover your new one.

Now, the reality is that you'll probably be doing this for the rest of your life. But the good news is that you'll become more and more aligned with your real life's purpose with each outgrowth of your old purpose and discovery of your new one.

So, if you've ever had doubts about your mission, know that it's normal. It's even natural to feel aimless for a while, as long as you don't stop looking. And as long as you keep searching, you'll grow closer and closer to uncovering your actual calling.

You might think being a good parent is your life’s purpose, which is an honorable purpose, but are you a good parent to your children?

Consistency and routine are important aspects of good parenting, as they provide children with a sense of control. Redundancy becomes the goal for parents as good parenting focuses on creating independence in children.

Parenting should be done in a way that takes into account the age and stage of development of the children. That is, there is a connection between children's developmental age and expectations, discipline, and resilience-building tactics.

The goal of good parenting is to socialize children. Parents give their children and teenagers social scripts to help them navigate their growing-up years. This social scripting aids them in navigating both online and offline environments.

Good parenting instills into children a growth perspective rather than a perspective that believes a child's intelligence is fixed. Parenting that fosters a growth mindset focuses on work and strategy rather than just recognizing and developing innate abilities.

Encouragement takes precedence over praise, consequences take precedence over punishment, and collaboration takes precedence over obedience in good parenting. This guarantees that parenting is appropriate for the times we live in.

Children should be expected to help around the house without being paid in order to learn to be givers rather than takers. Parenting is complicated, taking into account variances in birth order, personality, and gender. One size does not fit all when it comes to parenting.

The optimal parenting style, according to the best available research, is an authoritative style that is a balance of firmness and nurturing. When children are educated by parents who utilize an authoritative manner, the consequences are often better in terms of academic accomplishment, mental health, and overall well-being.

When families are directed by democracies or benign dictatorships, they function well. A family should have someone in charge, and it's ideal if it's the parents! What is the state of your parenting? What's it like to be a part of your family?

The following are some effective parenting strategies to guide you.

Listen to your child's words as words are powerful and meaningful. They try to tell you something from the minute they can speak.

Carve out time to eat together. Eating together is one of the top 10 ways to boost good energy, according to psychologists.

When disciplining your child, mean what you say. Don't say it in a mean way. When your child knows you will follow through and provide consequences for unfavorable behavior, you will not have to make idle threats of punishments.

Allow your child's accomplishments and failures to be theirs. Offer love, support, and praise where it is needed, but don't take over. As parents, we tend to want to control and fix everything, taking away the dignity or learning experience that is part of their journey.

Let's think about purpose in business or career. Have you set goals to run a successful business? Are you still looking for that big break? Is it your purpose to simply live a life that is not money-driven but just wanting to get by? Are you content? Do you feel like something is missing?

When you are living without a purpose, you have no idea what it is you are looking for, what you want in life, or what happiness you can achieve by finding and knowing what a life with purpose looks like. You may get out of bed and go to work, not feel fulfilled, go home, and still wonder what you're looking for. Although you have people around you who you care about and things you do that add temporary fun, a life without purpose is not meaningful. To exist each day knowing what that reason is and what purpose you are on this earth for will have you setting goals you never knew you were capable of doing.

What can you do to find your purpose? Rachel thought she was living a purposeful life when she was working at the exchange. It was a life in which she saw money and felt powerful. Then, one day, she decided it was all done. She felt she wanted and needed something more, but she couldn't figure out what it was.

This is what happens when you are going through life, without purpose and true meaning. Rachel was on top of the world. Why would she even think about her purpose when she was living the best life possible? She had moved into Center City Phila when she was just 20 years old, into an apartment with her friend, Sean. She had made it! She had a great job. She was dating around in the city. She was young and carefree and thought she had the world ahead of her, all the time in the world.

The feeling of power that came with the money was a feeling she could not explain, but she liked it more than anything she had ever felt in her life. A sense of security she never knew existed. Slowly, money became the focal point of her life. Not that it was a bad thing, but when you go after more and more, a time eventually comes when you stop enjoying the simpler things in life or even enjoy all the money you have earned with your blood and sweat.

One day her boss, Neil, came to her and said, *"Rachel, you have done such an amazing job. I want to reward you with a $15,000.00 bonus."*

"Are you kidding me?" She screamed.

Neil's face dropped because he thought Rachel wasn't happy with the bonus. He was quick to revise it and replied, *"Well, I will see if maybe we can get a little more for you."*

He didn't or couldn't understand Rachel at that point, who was so giddy with excitement because she had never seen this kind of money at one time in her entire life.

She was rich! Rachel, right there on the spot, said, *"Thank you... I quit."*

The man was so confused by this. He was sure she was upset by the annual bonus she just received.

Then she explained, *"You see, I have never had money like this, so I think I will stop working and move... I am quitting."*

He truly did not know how to respond to her, even though he was not only her boss but also a really good friend. He was going to miss her, but he also knew she was serious, and there was no stopping her. She was so young and hadn't experienced going away to college or having the kind of fun most kids were having at her age. She was mature and responsible. He knew she would be back when she soon ran out of money, so he offered her to go away for a year. He reiterated that she would still have a job if she came back. That's exactly what she did.

Rachel parted for a year, working odd jobs and getting by, and a year later, she came back to work with Neil. She jumped back into her job at the exchange, and although it was fun and exciting, and she was back to making money, there was something in her life that was still missing.

For a couple of years, the young lady would go through the motions of living life... working, partying with her friends, and having a good time. She was young, and this is what she was supposed to be doing. Right?

Rachel had a great friend circle and an amazing job, and she was back in another apartment in Society Hill Towers in Center City. She had everything people strive for to feel complete, but she felt something big was still missing.

Maybe it was children, or maybe it was time for her to stop dating around, find someone, and start a family, she often thought. Her compassion for children was undeniable. She had a niece, 'Little Rachel,' who she was able to spend a good amount of time with when she was little and loved to spoil her.

Little Rachel and Big Rachel were quite the pair. Big Rachel loved olives, and so she would teach little Rachel the *"octopus garden"* song by The Beatles by placing olives on every finger like an octopus. Every time Big Rachel would even hum the song, little Rachel would run to the fridge and get the olives! It was brilliant. Big Rachel adored little Rachel and wanted her own child. She started to think at the young age of 22 maybe that's what's missing.

Many people go through life unsure of what they truly desire. They usually blindly follow the American Dream since it is expected of them. That, in my opinion, is a terrible way to live one's life. To avoid seeming corny, I'd like to emphasize that you only have one life; make the most of it by doing things that make you happy. And you should get started immediately!

You are not alone if you don't know what you truly desire in life. Every day, tens of thousands, if not millions, of people roam aimlessly around the globe. If you don't want to waste your life wandering aimlessly, apply the recommendations below to figure out exactly what you want out of life.

If you consistently sacrifice your time and dreams for other people, you won't be able to pinpoint exactly what you want in life. It is necessary for you to prioritize yourself. Consider this question: What would you be doing right now if you weren't bound by your job, family, friends, or anything else? Always keep in mind that it's fine to prioritize yourself because no one else will.

Nothing should be regretted. Feel free to be self-centered. It's your life, and you're in charge of it. It's time for you to live it your way. You won't be able to go forward if you are continually regretting what you did or didn't do in the past. Don't go back in time. Live in the here and now... as well as in the future!

Determine what you require. Take a seat and consider what you require the most. Is it a member of your family? The ability to express yourself freely? Do you believe in love? Is your financial situation secure? Is there anything else?

It can be difficult to determine what you require at times. Sit down and determine which elements of your life require greater attention and what is preventing you from living the life you desire. After that, you can construct a priority list. Also, consider what kind of legacy you wish to leave.

Figure out what is bothering you the most. Only by fighting back against something you don't want can you soar. Figure out what irritates you and be explicit. Don't simply state that you despise your office job. Determine why you despise it. Is it possible that your micromanaging employer is to blame?

What is the nature of your work? What's the point of your worthless job title? Or a combination of the two? What's bothering you, and what can you do about it? How much do you want to spend to get it fixed?

Determine what truly makes you happy. There is no such thing as a waste of life if you are content to live it. Your desires are rooted in your satisfaction. So, spend a few minutes reflecting on what makes you happy. Is it a journey? Being in the presence of children? Do you want to run a profitable business? What is the name of your significant other? Is it possible to be financially independent?

You'll have a clear sense of what you should strive for in your life once you've identified the one thing that makes you the happiest. Rachel's thoughts traveled to the present, as she reflected what kind of life the woman had led so far. The time spent at the exchange with her colleagues and friends was the highlight of her life.

But now, when they were no more and when that old life was no more, Rachel knew she had to find a way to live again. A life of purpose and meaning. She had to find it for the people who lost their lives.

Chapter 5 - Piece of Me

*"Carve your name on hearts, not tombstones. A legacy is etched into the minds of others and the stories they share about you." **-Shannon L. Alder***

What does it mean to be remembered? Or to leave a legacy behind? It entails leaving an imprint on the future and contributing to future generations. People want to feel that their lives matter; thus, they want to leave a legacy.

Why do people feel as if leaving behind a legacy is important? Here are a few reasons:

Part of the Ongoing Foundation of Life

Those who have gone before us have left us with the world we live in. Those who follow us will only have what we leave behind. We are stewards of this earth and have a responsibility to leave it in a better state than we found it, even if our contribution seems very little.

Raw Power for Both Good and Bad

There have been people who have positively impacted the globe, who have opened up new worlds for millions of others, and who have inspired others to achieve new heights. On the other hand, there are those who have wreaked havoc on countless millions of people, leaving a trail of misery in their wake. There are parents who have bestowed excellence onto their children and parents who have damaged their children's delicate brains and souls. What we do has an impact on others. Our life has the ability to bring about either good or harm. It is critical that we make the decision to do good. Rachel found this to be so important in her life. She wanted her kids to live a life with values and integrity. She tried to make sure her children had the best possible life. They were to live an extension of the wonderful life she had built for herself and her husband and not feel as though because they were young, they were not deserving of all the same things.

James, Jess, and Jojo were never spoiled but had the best of everything. They always showed appreciation for the things they were given. Rachel's children, at a very young age, would gather their toys to give to those less fortunate and join her in walking the streets and feeding the homeless when they were older. Christmas after Christmas, she watched her kids look in excitement as someone opened a gift one of her kids was presenting them because, just like her, they would much rather give than receive.

Act of Responsibility to Leave a Legacy Behind

It is a huge responsibility to choose to leave a positive legacy because of the power of our life and the legacies we leave. All decent men and women must accept responsibility for leaving legacies that will propel the future generation to heights we can only dream of. Having a core element of our life centered on the objective of leaving a legacy is a big part of what makes us decent and decent individuals.

Breaks the Pull of Selfishness That Is Present in All of Us

When we work to leave a legacy, we are working in a selfless manner that can benefit everyone. Yes, someone may work hard to gain money so that when they die, a building will be named after them, but that is not the type of legacy we are discussing. We're talking about leaving behind legacies that improve the lives of people who follow after us, not about glory or notoriety for ourselves, but about helping others.

After all, we won't be around to see our legacy come to fruition. Building something that will outlast us is unselfish, and living with that in mind removes the power of selfishness, which strives so hard to infiltrate our lives.

Keeps Us Focused on the Big Picture

Building a legacy is an important aspect of the "big picture." It helps us stay focused in the long term and provides us with values by which we can evaluate our activities. We are concentrating on the "small picture;" whatever is feasible right now when we behave based on selfishness, personal expediency, and the like.

We are considering a "large vision" while we are creating a life that will live for many years. Consider the following questions: How will this action affect my overall objectives? What impact will this have on individuals in the future? How important is it to leave a legacy behind? How important is THAT legacy left behind to the world and the ones who loved and cared about us when we were alive? How will we be remembered? How do we want to be remembered? All of these questions came to Rachel, at every waking moment of her days, after 9/11, and after the day she found out how fickle life really is.

To Rachel, it meant the world. The importance of leaving something behind was so important! She used to ponder day and night about what she was doing that was making a difference and what she *could* be doing instead. She had started working on a legacy long before she knew it. Maybe she began working on her legacy as a child and leaving a message to those less fortunate.

What was the message? To not let anything stand in their way of success. She had worked so hard from the age of 14 and never stopped working to achieve her goals. It was something that had to count, right? Maybe her legacy continued as a teen when she saw a homeless man, eating food at her very own table. Here, she learned the importance of extending your hand to those in need whenever you see someone and not turning your back. She wanted her legacy to be known as someone who, as a mother, made sure her kids KNEW she would always be there in their time of need financially, emotionally, and physically to help them through their life struggles. The bond she learned to form with them and the acceptance of exactly who each of them is as individuals carry her legacy of an understanding woman. Her legacy shares the pain she needed to feel when she ended a 22-year marriage and acceptance that she could not save one of the people she had loved so much, her very own husband. She learned how to help others struggling to save someone in addiction. She learned so many life lessons to pass down well beyond her journey.

She knows she leaves a piece of herself within each of her children. Her powerful drive to be successful shines through in her son, James. Her determination to never give up and to have the ability to rise above any challenges to be able to help others is displayed in her daughter's actions. Her courage to stand alone, not needing help from others, showing great leadership qualities is one that is carried on through her son, Joe.

She leaves behind a legacy of kindness, compassion, generosity, and great accomplishments in the face of adversity. She wants her kids to remember her as funny and someone who maybe adds a little more excitement when she told them stories. It was just her way. They always told her she has quite a way to embellish everything she says. At the lowest point of her life, in Halifax, all she could think about were the three most important things in her life — her children. She thought of the amazing trips they had taken together and the fun they had. She thought about how they had just gone to Euro Disney in France a month before. The excitement they had all felt moving to London. She was so worried about the kids fitting in, but it was a weightless concern. Her kids fit in just fine. Within a few weeks, she loved watching James running down the street with some local boys playing soccer. Jess would always be playing in the yard with two little girls, Izzy and Emma. And Joseph, or Jojo as they called him, would be running around the backyard yelling out what would be his first word which was 'airplane.'

It was going to be great for the family thinking back. But after what she had been through, she was returning as a completely different person. She was struggling so hard to be the mother they needed her to be, but her life as she knew it had crumbled with those towers, and she was an empty shell of sadness and regret — a person full of guilt and someone who was trying to hold it together.

Rachel was still struggling so hard to discover why God hadn't taken her on 9/11. The overwhelming sense of guilt had consumed her day in and day out. She was certain there was a greater purpose she should be serving. What did God want her to do?

Was there something great waiting for her or was death going to come back and get her? She struggled with the idea for a long time. The deathly day that took all her friends missed her, and one day it was sure to come back and take her too. She was almost waiting for it to happen.

"We leave something of ourselves behind when we leave a place; we stay there, even though we go away. And there are things in us that we can find again only by going back there." ***-Pascal Mercier, Night Train to Lisbon***

Maybe all she wanted to do was make a mark on the world and leave a piece of herself behind, for people to benefit from - her family, children, and friends to take pride in.

What was the purpose of leaving her here? She asked this question every morning when she woke up. Through the most trying times in her life, she would ask, *what I have learned from this and how I can help others from what I have learned.*

She knew she would have to face the families of her lost friends, and how could she make them feel any better? She would have to try.

The desire or need to be remembered for what you have done to the world is the concept of leaving a legacy. In certain circumstances, that contribution is so unique that it permanently alters the cosmos.

Most mere mortals, on the other hand, will leave a more modest legacy, one that may not necessarily transform the world but does make a lasting impression on those whose lives you have touched.

Here are some ways to leave a great legacy:

Reflect and Decide What Is the Most Important Thing in Your Life

Several thoughts may come to mind when you reflect on your life's journey. Did you develop and maybe transform your life, make adjustments when necessary, realize your truth, inspire others, become a leader, or influence others? Living a pleasant and purposeful life requires touching lives and exemplifying a true path. Your name will be remembered for a long time.

Be a Mentor to Others

By definition, a mentor is a more experienced or skilled individual in a certain field. Everyone has something important to say to others that will help less experienced individuals navigate through life. Personal growth and support are important aspects of the mentoring-mentee relationship. This process entails an information exchange, as well as psychological and/or social support, which is critical for maintaining new attitudes. Even when the mentee has moved on to influence others, these ties may endure a lifetime.

Pursue Your Passion because They Are Important

Your interests will leave an indelible mark on the world. Passion is the result of an outpouring of interests and ideas that have a positive impact on your life. You may see your destiny clearly if you find and pursue your passion. If you don't follow your hobbies to the utmost, life will be boring. It's spreadable. It's a religious thing. Don't give up the chance to pursue your hobbies and then seek out new adventures. A significant portion of your life's job is to leave a legacy. A life committed to self-reflection and purpose leaves a legacy. An honest and value-driven body of life will be disclosed and will survive.

Leave the Gift of Education Behind

You know how they say that if you give a man a fish, he'll eat for a day, but if you teach him to fish, he'll eat for a lifetime. It is unquestionably correct. Teaching others is one of the most useful things you can do. The great part is that you're not only directly assisting someone but also setting the stage for a domino effect. The individual you assist may be able to aid others in turn, ensuring that your knowledge and ability are passed on even further.

Contribute to the Society

Our knowledge and ideas are significant gifts to leave behind, but they aren't the only ones we may leave. What comes to mind when you think about philanthropy? Perhaps you think of well-known examples of charity, such as Bill Gates' and Warren Buffet's large donations. This may make generosity appear unattainable or unreasonable. You don't have to be a millionaire to have an impact. Smaller gestures, such as planting trees and digging wells in areas where they are needed, have a huge impact on people's lives. What things in your life can you point out, may it be qualities, achievements, memories, when it comes to leaving behind a legacy? What do you want people to know about you? How do you want them to remember you? How will you make sure people know how important they are to you? Pondering on these questions will help you create a blueprint for what you CAN do to make sure your legacy lives on.

Chapter 6 – You Are in Charge

"Your journey is completely yours. It is unique. Others may try to steal part of it, tell it in their words, or shape it to suit them. Reality is no one can live it or own it but you. Take charge of your journey. It's yours and yours alone!" ***—Kemi Sogunle, author***

Have you ever heard the phrase "My life, my rules"? The statement carries the core of the idea — your life is in your hands. It was popularized by viral posts and memes on the internet.

One's life and fate are frequently under one's control. One's actions and decisions determine one's fate. Taking control of one's life can help people find their way in life. No one else has the authority to make decisions for you that will lead you along the road you desire. That power is solely in the hands of the person.

No matter what obstacles you face or who you enlist to assist you during difficult times, only you have the power to guide your life in the way you choose. Always remember this ultimate truth. When was the last time that you felt completely in charge of the decisions and actions presented to you?

Can you think of a specific time of your life when you felt completely in charge? What did that look like? Were you a small child deciding for yourself, *"I will not eat that vegetable, and you can't make me!"* Or were you a camp counselor keeping lots of little children busy and happy, and you felt you had it all under control? Maybe you are the CEO of a Fortune 500 company and therefore are in charge of a lot of people.

Sometimes, being in charge can be so overwhelming, we lose control and sight of who we are. We don't like to face the fact that we may have failed or even think about the possibility of failure. We find it easier to shift the blame elsewhere for things that may go wrong, and therefore we allow our circumstances, whatever they may be, to lead us toward a life where we feel unsatisfied.

Have you ever wondered why, when we make a mistake or face a challenge in life, some individuals begin to blame everyone around them? An unknown author once said, *"The world's greatest wars are waged within one's soul's silent chambers."*

What could this possibly mean? We tend to hang on to bad beliefs about ourselves within these metaphorical chambers. We have a tendency to cling to all of our regrets, failures, and what-ifs in life, resulting in a completely different picture of ourselves than what we attempt to present to others.

Many of us are constantly berating ourselves for previous mistakes. This feeling can use our lives to spiral in directions we are unhappy about. Simply said, blaming someone else is far simpler than accepting complete responsibility for your actions. It's also simpler to point the finger at someone else rather than examine why we made the mistake we did and face the repercussions, whether it was something you did at work or something that occurred during a fight with your partner. It takes less work to transfer blame and is easier on our emotions, at least in the short term.

Blaming others is a defensive technique. It's referred to as denial or projection because it helps us maintain our feeling of self-esteem or pride by preventing us from seeing our problems. What is the solution to this problem?

Accepting Responsibility of Our Actions and Decisions

Accepting responsibility comprises two parts. Let's start with the first one: embracing personal responsibility, which is taking responsibility for your actions and the consequences of those actions. It will be impossible for you to acquire self-esteem or even have the respect of others unless you accept responsibility for your actions or failings.

It is a basic fact that all humans (young and old) make errors and terrible decisions. It's the same when we don't act when we know we should. There are moments when we all turn a blind eye when we know what the correct thing to do is to aid.

So, first and foremost, you should recognize that you are not the first (and will not be the last) individual to make mistakes in terms of personal behavior.

Indirect responsibility is the second part of taking accountability. It entails going beyond oneself and taking action to aid individuals or circumstances in your immediate environment that require assistance. While indirect responsibility does not equal personal accountability, it does tell something about your character and personality.

Clearly, many people will pass by the individual who is homeless or down on his or her luck on the street. Others, thankfully, will soon come to a halt and provide assistance. It's not difficult to figure out which of these two options is the most responsible one.

When the chance to make a good or terrible choice presents itself, the actual difference between being responsible and being irresponsible is an indicator of how well we're managing our lives. Accepting responsibility for one's actions, both direct and indirect, is one essential aspect in determining one's real character. When that critical time arrives, what you do or don't do reveals the true nature of the person you are.

On rare occasions or in the near term, refusing to accept personal responsibility may work in your favor. You might be able to get away with keeping your mouth shut about whatever you've done or even putting your wrongdoing on someone else. You may not be held accountable for your wrongdoings at the time.

However, make no mistake about it. This terrible decision will ultimately come up with you, and it will almost always cause you more grief in the long run than if you had faced the problem head-on, accepted responsibility, and honestly stated, *"I did it."*

"When you blame others, you give up your power to change." ***-Anonymous***

Rachel's mother accepted responsibility for herself and her actions when Rachel was 16. She went, got help, and became sober. This extremely brave act changed the future of the entire family. Things became more stable in Rachel's home. Her mom showed interest in everything she was doing.

You could see the woman wanted so badly to find the magic words to make the past disappear and give her a chance at a real future with her kids. She was full of guilt from the life she may have led but also full of gratitude for finding a program to help her. She used every tool in the box to continue forward and eventually help others in the family find their way to sobriety. She is a truly remarkable, beautiful person. That's what you get when you accept responsibility!

What Happens If We Don't Accept Responsibility?

Accepting responsibility has serious implications over time. It has a terrible impact on your mind and heart, first and foremost. When you realize you haven't taken responsibility for something you should, it starts to worry you and gnaw at you. You'll quickly realize how little you are on the inside.

That may appear to be a stretch, but it's the truth. Taking responsibility for your behaviors improves life. Remember that self-respect is the estimation of your worth or value.

As a result of your continued refusal to accept personal responsibility, you will eventually ensure that you will see your life as having little to no actual value.

"A man can do what he ought to do, and when he says he cannot, it's because he will not." ***-J. A. Froude***

We don't always recognize the long-term consequences of our actions, especially when we're young. But make no mistake, taking personal and indirect responsibility is a key component in earning respect and admiration for people around you. Accepting responsibility is not only the proper thing to do, but it will also pay you in more ways than you may think in the long run.

*"In the long run, we shape our lives, and we shape ourselves. The process never ends until we die. And the choices we make are ultimately our own responsibility." **-Eleanor Roosevelt***

The Art of Surrendering Control

Sometimes, the strongest thing we CAN do is let go of control, especially when things aren't going our way. Rachel understood the importance of surrendering her control when she couldn't change the bad or wrong things in her life. But the 'how' came much later.

Once done, she noticed how smoothly her life went by when she gave up control and allowed things to happen instead of making them happen. It was a very difficult thing for her to learn, master, and do. She was a control freak who so often used her energy trying to plan, predict, and prevent things that nobody could possibly plan, predict, or even prevent. She knew very well that she had to give up control in her marriage and let go. She had to admit she was powerless. She had to walk away.

It was a great marriage for many years filled with laughter and love. They had first met at a dance club, and it was instant love followed by marriage six months later. Both she and Joe shared a love for travel and adventure, and when her job took off, he was there to be Mr. mom to their kids.

It just worked. She could pursue her career in finance, and he would stay home. He didn't mind the role reversal, and she was just starting to make good money. They had a summer house in Ocean City, NJ, and a beautiful home in Marlboro, NJ. Life was good. They had also purchased lots of toys - Porsches and Corvettes, jet-skis, a boat, and a Harley Davidson motorcycle that all sat in the garage.

Things were great, and they had a lot of fun with their kids. They had lots of friends and would often have BBQs and parties with their kids' friends and parents at their house. The parties would usually end with someone's parent asleep on the front lawn from drinking too much, and they would all have a laugh.

Rachel and Marylou became lifelong best friends when they met and realized they shared the same values and undeniable love for their children. They loved to have neighborhood parties. After football games on Sunday or a Friday night, they would gather Jackie, Erin, Debbie, and their spouses for really fun times. They were all quite a crew while the kids were growing up, and all the kids loved being together. They had really fun times. Rachel and Marylou's families were like one big family. They took lots of vacations together and looked after each other in times of need.

Being a mother was Rachel's greatest joy in life. With each child born, she felt more complete. The infant stage was her favorite. When she would hold one of the kids in her arms and knew they needed her for EVERYTHING, it made her feel strong, especially when she held Joseph, who was 11 lbs. at birth!

She was not a mom who followed a strict schedule because she worked and needed to make sure she had time with her children. Sometimes the babies would be awake at 10 p.m., and she would get five hours of sleep before going back to work, but she loved every second of it.

As the kids grew older, they became very self-sufficient. James was cooking breakfast for himself at the age of 10. Joseph decided, one day, he was ready to ride a bike, so he went outside, got on, and taught himself. Jessica was always helping her little brother and around the house. She loved to bake with Rachel.

Working so many hours during the week left her trying so hard to make up time on the weekends with her kids. Anything they wanted to do, she would go and do it. She tried to make the time they spent together count.

Rachel and Joe took lots of trips together and had plenty of date nights without the kids. The kids, on their part, liked going to their grandma, Dottie's house, who would hide gems in the backyard, and they would have to find them. She even let them build a fire in her fireplace so they would never seem to mind a sleepover at grandma's. They just really enjoyed each other's company. Joe and Rachel loved their family. When had it all gone wrong?

On one trip to South Beach, Joe wasn't feeling well and went to the hospital. They diagnosed him with bronchitis and sent him back to the hotel. The couple was there with some friends, so they went about their night, and Joe hung in there even though he was not feeling very good.

The next morning, he said, *"I am really struggling to breathe here."*

At the same time, they noticed a message on the hotel phone. It was from the hospital and said, *"We misdiagnosed you... please come back immediately; your lung is collapsed... do NOT get on a plane."*

The news was so shocking. Joe ran out of the room as fast as he could and back to Mt. Sinai, Miami.

Rachel followed right behind her husband, dazed and confused with what was going on but determined to see nothing happened to him. She packed up their bags, all the while thinking, *"Sure, this was all a misunderstanding,"* and headed to the hospital.

They would head home from there. When she arrived at the hospital and took one glance at her husband, Rachel knew by the green color of his face and the tube coming out of his chest that it was bad. Very bad!

Weeks later, he was released from the hospital. They boarded a train as he couldn't fly and went home. The first doctor the couple saw back in NJ handed Joe 50 Dilaudid and 30 Percocet in case the Dilaudid didn't do the trick. It was the beginning of the end of life, as the family knew it. This was a battle they would fight together for the next eight years - a battle so intense you needed strong armor and an army of strong will and desire to enter the war. If one person gave up control in this battle, everyone was taken down, so after many tries for a victory, Rachel admitted defeat. Finally, after years, she admitted that she couldn't change anything. Things weren't in her control. Nothing was in her control. As a result, their long and fruitful marriage ended.

Today, Rachel has taken control back in her life and remains powerless over others. She finds gratitude in the situation she is in, as it has helped her lend a hand to those in similar situations who may be feeling hopeless. She respects Joe and doesn't feel the need to blame him for how any part of her journey has turned out. Instead, she believes it was by God's will that her life turned out the way it did - every part. Similarly, we are all in control of our life. From that child who starts to say NO to the adult who chooses path A or path B, it is up to us.

The speed of life has increased to the point that many of us are unable to adjust completely. As a result, we live in a constant state of concern that we aren't doing what we're supposed to be doing, and the anxiety we experience makes it harder to get things done, leading to a cycle of inactivity.

More agency is what we need - the capacity to cut through all of the pulls on us, achieve emotional and physical balance, think more clearly, and advocate for ourselves so that we can take the best course of action. We might feel more in control of our life when we have agency.

How to take responsibility for your actions while being in control of your life?

Listen to Your Inner Voice – It Always Guides Right

You have a distinct soul imprint and a distinct "purpose" from everyone else on the earth. It might be a single large goal or, more likely, a wonderful jigsaw of smaller goals that come together to form a beautiful image of your life. If you want to figure out your life's purpose and what you genuinely desire, you must learn to seek guidance and assistance from your mind and spirit.

Start by meditating, soul writing, reading, dancing, spending time in nature, and getting lost in the flow of the activities you like to strengthen your connection with your inner spirit.

Draw a Map of What You Desire

If you don't know where you're going, you could wind up exactly where you're going, which isn't where you want to be.

In all key life areas, from love, friendships, livelihood, finances, health, spirituality, fun, and leisure, write down your dreams, goals, values, and how you want to feel in your life.

Not only will this provide you with a goal to strive for, but the universe will also begin to provide you with people, things, and events that correspond to what you've described Rachel went is search of this connection with her inner spirit, and decided to explore a camp she heard about. It was called Camp Powerment. Within thirty minutes of arriving at camp, Rachel's friendships with her "Camp friends" began to blossom. She had met some of the most amazing women. However, she had no idea who they were outside of camp, or what they did for a living. This truly incredible program designed by the camp owner, Tammy Leader, her beloved mother Grandy, and daughter Chelsea was full of fun, healing, learning, and growth for women from all walks of life. It was perfected so everyone was able to get to know each other for exactly who they were, not who they needed to be in society. It was brilliant! Rachel finished a long weekend at camp with clarity to go forward on her personal journey and with many amazing new friends. A particular group of women, made up of Rachel, Marcy, Lori, Vicki and Susan who Rachel likes to call "The fabulous Five", never let too much time go before planning a weekend away or a simple get together for a day. They know how lucky they are to have each other. It was nature and the universe that brought them together at this fabulous camp and they are sisters for life.

Start Believing and Living Your Dreams Today

Rather than waiting for a day in the future when you'll be miraculously transported into the life of your dreams, think about how you may start living your dreams right now. Buy an inexpensive canvas and paint kit and set aside a Saturday afternoon to paint if you want to feel creative.

Reach a buddy, plan a long weekend stroll, enroll in a yoga class, or bookmark nutritious recipes online if you want to feel healthy and alive.

Take yourself out on a solo date, wear matching underwear, have a massage, or make a list of all the things you like about yourself to feel loved and attractive.

Try to Remain More Present

The majority of us only live around 10% of our lives. We spend the remaining 90% of our time buried in our heads, obsessed with previous memories, circular ideas, and anxieties about the future, or judgments and responses to what we see. Alternatively, we may be engrossed in our cellphones and television screens.

We are not truly connected to the vitality, beauty, and enchantment of the world around us, nor are we grounded in our bodies and minds. We're missing out on our lives, leaving us feeling shallow, hollow, and uneasy.

Attempt to be more present during the day. If you can do it, do it every hour. Consider how your clothes feel on your skin, the breeze in the air, the noises around you, the taste and fragrance of your meal, the sun or rain, the beauty of a flower, the touch of a loved one, and the sensations of your body as you walk, cook, or dance. When you're present, you're in command, you're in all of your majesty and authority. Not only do you get to enjoy the richness of life, but you also get to select how you react to situations rather than reacting on auto-pilot. Instead of being dominated by your ideas and emotions, you learn to become the queen/king of your mind. While doing all of the above, also think of what you want to leave behind after you are gone. What do you want your legacy to look like? Because if you know it or not, you are creating your legacy every day. The great things you do for people, the not-so-great things you do when you are having a bad day, are all part of your legacy. Maybe you would like to buy a 100 good deeds bracelet at www.100gooddeeds.org as a reminder to do a good deed. Or maybe you want to donate some of your books to a library in a war-torn country or sponsor a school, where some part of you will remain long after you are gone.

That act of kindness goes a long way and helps you leave a legacy to be proud of. Building a legacy is the only way to leave a lasting mark, whether you want to improve the world's energy use, eliminate poverty, or save the Amazon forest. A legacy establishes your life's work as something that will benefit future generations, even though you will never see it realized. It's a desire to build something bigger than oneself, something that will benefit the planet indefinitely. A legacy is a gift you leave behind without expecting a return, much like a farmer who plants an apple tree, knowing he'll never reap the benefits of the orchard. Consider Martin Luther King Jr.'s contributions to civil rights, Thomas Edison's contributions to electricity, or Margaret Sanger's contributions to women's health care.

They died before their legacies were fully realized, yet their contributions to society will always be remembered.

A legacy is more than a task. It isn't something that happens overnight. You may leave an indelible impact on the world if you connect with your genuine purpose and establish your legacy through commitment, hard effort, and meaningful contribution.

Chapter 7 – Kill Them with Kindness

*"Guard well within yourself that treasure, kindness. Know how to give without hesitation, how to lose without regret, how to acquire without meanness." –**George Sand***

Kindness is a word that carries so much weight, yet it is often overlooked and lost in the midst of our fast-paced contemporary lives. It is perhaps the most fundamental thing in nature. Even without language and coherence, societies and civilizations, knowledge, fame, and power, kindness existed, persisted, and thrived. It is the most basic form of communication between animals and humans alike, something that everyone understands before we ever even learn how to speak. It resides in the smallest of acts but makes the biggest of differences.

*"Life is mostly froth and bubble. Two things stand like stone. Kindness in another's trouble, courage in your own." —**Adam Lindsay Gordon***

When you think of kindness, perhaps what comes to your mind is only someone who is generous, or perhaps someone who is selfless all the time, but that's not what kindness is. Kindness isn't just about doing big acts of altruism, and it certainly isn't about making public statements about giving to the charity. It's really about those small, momentary, and impulsive acts of helping someone out or wanting to brighten up someone's day. It is the smile you give to the lovely old lady across the street as you pass by her house in the morning. It is the way you stop your car in the middle of the road to allow a trail of baby ducks to waddle across with their mama. It is the way a random child wraps their whole hand around your finger and looks at you so you can take their balloon down from the tree, and you do it just because you can.

It is the way you compliment a lady's dress who smiles despite having a bad day. It is the way you stop on an empty road to help the family whose car broke down in the middle of their trip. It is the subtle pat on the back of your employee to let them know they're doing a good job. It is the silent hug you give to a person who has suffered a great loss.

It is the faith of a hurt, stray cat who reluctantly comes to you when you offer her food. It is the trust of a blind man who holds onto you as you help him across the street. It is the grateful smile of the pregnant lady as you move to give her your seat. Kindness is all of the things that make you human. It is compassion and goodwill; it is love in the purest of its forms.

People show this compassion in many different ways. Some choose to show their kindness through compliments and verbal affirmations, while some people who are not that vocal choose to spread their positive energy via their actions, whether it be a small smile or a genuine hug, or even helping someone out. It also differs between introverted and extroverted people. While extroverted people might appreciate public gestures of kindness, introverted people might not. This is because introverted people are often shy and might feel mortified if you try to give them a gift in public or compliment them when you're in a large crowd of people since this will draw attention to them only. Extroverted people, on the other hand, might not mind that attention. Knowing and understanding the personalities of the ones around you can only improve your bond with them.

With the rise of COVID-19, more and more people have forgotten what kindness is. The quarantine period has taken away all our opportunities to show this compassion to one another. Nobody can pass on a genuine smile with their masks on, nobody can give a hug while staying six feet away, and nobody can touch one another to let them know how they feel. Touch is a huge part of kindness, like patting one on the back, touching their arm in a reassuring way, or holding someone's hand out of love. You couldn't even compliment random strangers on the street because you barely saw any people around. As the world makes its move back toward normalcy, it has become important, now more than ever, to remind ourselves to be kind toward each other. Over the years, we have only become more and more divided. We've allowed our religious, political, social, racial, and linguistic differences to come between us and cause a rift in our path toward betterment. It almost feels as though kindness has been sucked out of this world for good, so it is a good time to put it back in again.

We need to get back out into society and meet new people. We need to watch out for our neighbors and get back together with friends. We just need to go back to loving each other regardless of what we do and believe. It doesn't hurt to make one small kind gesture a day.

The field Rachel chose to work in isn't one where you feel a lot of kindness spread throughout the day. The people work at a fast, competitive, get-your-job-done pace. It's a stressful environment where there are deals to be done, and timing is everything. No one is chit-chatting at the coffee machine. You eat lunch while you speak to your clients, and they are doing the same. It's a long 10-hour day where you give it all you get and go home. Her clients must know her well, and trust her judgment, and she works very hard to ensure they do. She has built a friendship with many clients over the years.

Although they work in a stressful environment day in day out, the generosity these people show is just amazing. The kindness that is expressed by the bankers and brokers alike is above and beyond any generosity one could ever ask for in a time of need.

Rachel's friend, Dave, won a bunch of N90 masks at a charity event in a silent auction. You would think that would be a good thing to hold on to for your family during a pandemic, but his kindness had him pick up the phone and call her. He soon donated those to Rachel's friend, an Emergency Room doctor, and his colleagues at downtown NY Presbyterian Hospital in NYC. Just one of the kind and generous acts she witnessed while knowing these bankers.

Rachel walked 60 miles for breast cancer and had to raise $2500 to do so. Not only did they fund her walk, but her client's wife, Carissa, also went on to fund her sister Tracy's entire walk through her company's charitable contribution.

Anytime there was a cause, Rachel just needed to get the word out and knew all her clients would be in. Each year for the 9/11 charity alone, millions of dollars are raised to go to many charities. It makes Rachel and her colleagues so proud to be a part of raising money for so many great causes.

In 2011, Rachel had a stroke. She needed to have surgery on her heart. The doctor told her it was to close a hole that she had, allowing clots to go through. It was a very scary time. The night before the surgery, she was surrounded at home by her family when a car pulled up out front. Her client, Mick, got out of the car and came to visit with her. He just wanted to make sure she was okay and let her know he was there for her. This is what it is like for Rachel. She knew her clients well and considered them her friends.

Rachel knew it was very important to show gratitude for such generous acts. Being genuinely thankful is also a big part of kindness since it is this humble gratitude that really allows a simple act of kindness to touch your heart. People forget that, and instead of being grateful, they sometimes dismiss the act or even look at it with a skeptic lens. Instead of building trust, this only breeds annoyance in the hearts of people.

This was very common in her work field, so Rachel always tried to be kind and spread kindness. She tried to teach the same to people who she mentored. She liked to think that this was a part of who she was, and it was a big part. Just like other parents, she wanted her kids to remember their mother as the person who, in a field where no one even appreciates another, says, *"Hey, you did a really good job today."*

"Treat everyone with politeness and kindness, not because they are nice, but because you are." ***-Roy T. Bennett, The Light in the Heart***

Even if you come out into the world and see that kindness has been lost, you should be the one to take the first step. Always remember that the good that you do will always have a ripple effect. All it takes is one person and one small act of love to eventually start a chain reaction. The good that you do always goes around.

This is because when someone is kind to us, we often feel the need to pay it forward. If not that, it definitely puts a smile on our faces. That's all it takes for a person's mood to become better and for their heart to soften up. There have been many instances when Rachel experienced this before, when people have been kind to her, and she felt the need to pay it forward and be kind to someone else, like the time when the residents of Halifax came to the motocross raceway to help the passengers of the plane out when they had landed in their country.

Sometimes certain experiences also make us want to be kind to one another. This is because our ability to relate to others plays a big role in allowing us to connect with other people. This connectedness gives us a sense of responsibility. For instance, when somebody goes through something you have experienced, you go to lengths to ensure that nobody ends up in that same place you did. Your ability to relate to their pain makes you want to protect them, be kind to them, and just help them out.

Rachel met a woman named Sari who was going through a painful divorce. The two met through mutual friends at a beach bar. It wasn't long before they knew they were going to be in each other's lives. Through kindness and caring they became great friends. Rachel started out wanting to share her experience with Sari in hopes she would embrace her future and live in the moment as Rachel had learned. Going through a similar experience and finding a connection gave these two strangers the ability to become great friends.

This is why it is often said that trauma sometimes binds people together. It reminds people that whatever they are going through, they aren't alone. Maybe, this is what makes us humans so complex. We just find it in our hearts to be good to someone we barely even know just because we can relate to them on a certain level. It is this constant circulation of trust that allows us to function as a society and grow together. Another thing about kindness is that it isn't just meant for others. It is important to remember that we deserve the same love and consideration that we so easily give to other people. Sometimes people forget that, and it takes a toll on their mental well-being. This is why the next time you are kind to someone else, you must remind yourself to be kind to yourself too. You must remind yourself to take out time and treat yourself, go out, buy yourself some ice cream, do skincare, take a long bath, stay in and watch a movie, or even just try to get a good night's rest.

Our lives are increasingly becoming more and more challenging by the day. The world is moving too fast, and we are finding it hard to catch up. We are so busy chasing our goals that we forget to cherish these small moments of peace, and we don't even take the time out to look after ourselves. Make the decision today to always stop and remind yourself to take a break, catch a breath, and then move on to take the next step.

Like a wise man once said, *"Attitude is a choice. Happiness is a choice. Optimism is a choice. Kindness is a choice. Giving is a choice. Respect is a choice. Whatever choice you make, makes you. Choose wisely."* ***—Roy T. Bennett***

Choose to Be Kind Every Single Day!

Don't just do it when it is easy, do it when it is hard, do it unceasingly and incessantly. Give love because it is the one thing that you can give without any limitation. It is the one thing that can make a person's day so much better. Be kind, even when you don't receive kindness in return. Be kind, even to the person who despises you relentlessly. Send a smile their way every other day and watch how it softens their heart. Share your positive energy with other people. Give out random pieces of advice.

Rachel, too, was very good at showing kindness. It was who she was, and it all came naturally to her. It wasn't something she ever had to work at. When her children were little, she would try her best to make them feel special. She wanted each child to feel as though they were her favorite because they were each in their own way. She worked an awful lot, and she knew that, so, on the weekends, she would try to make up for it by doing what the kids wanted to do.

She would take them on little day trips to the park or overnight trips to Great Wolf Lodge or a water park, and sometimes on big trips on cruises or to an island. As the kids got older, she was able to go to even further places with them - places like Costa Rica and Iceland. One of her favorite trips was going to Bali with her son, Joe. He loved experiencing the culture and meeting the local people as much as she did.

Rachel's kids truly loved to travel as much as she did. Her time with her kids was her most favorite time spent. She was a kind and generous mother. One thing she liked to do that was very special to her was each year on their birthdays, she would make the biggest deal about it. It was truly their special day, and she wanted them to know it. The house would be decorated, lots of kids would come, and she would create fun games, have lots of food, and make a great party for her children.

She was also a kind, generous, and loving daughter and sister. If anyone in her family ever needed anything, she would rush to be there. She always felt that her good fortune was everyone's good fortune, so she was always willing to help anyone out who may have needed it.

One special birthday of her father, Rachel talked her siblings into surprising him with a new car. There was a party happening inside the house for her dad, Billy, when all of a sudden, he was called to go out front. Rachel and her sisters, their spouses, and kids stretched across the sidewalk like a big long wall and when they parted, behind them stood a shiny brand-new Green Jeep.

Billy's eyes lit up, and he went running toward the shiny vehicle with tears running down his face like it was the nicest thing anyone had ever done for him. That act of kindness and love didn't only warm his heart. But it also warmed all of their hearts that they could make someone so happy!

Do not just tell people that the world could be a better place; show them that. Show them that the change will only start with you. Kindness is something that you do, not to attain something in return, but out of pure unconditional love. You do it out of the wellness of your heart and out of the distinctiveness of your mind. You do it just to see someone smile. And you are thankful that you could help someone, even if it was just to smile.

*"Gratitude is the fairest blossom that springs from the soul." –**Henry Ward***

According to any dictionary you pick up, the meaning of gratitude is 'feeling or showing an appreciation of kindness; being thankful.' Where there is kindness, gratitude usually follows.

Gratitude is the act of expressing gratitude for what one has. It is an acknowledgment of value that is not based on monetary value. It is an expression of goodness and warmth that arises spontaneously from within. This social feeling deepens bonds and has strong evolutionary foundations, stemming from the survival benefit of assisting others and receiving assistance in return.

Gratitude is a natural emotion, but research is increasingly demonstrating its worth as a practice. That is, making deliberate attempts to acknowledge one's benefits. According to studies, people can intentionally nurture appreciation, and there are significant social and personal benefits to doing so. It is possible to be grateful to family, friends, co-workers, animals, nature, and life in general. The feeling creates a positive atmosphere that stretches both inside and outside.

Is Gratitude an Emotion?

Gratitude is a positive emotion that makes people happy. Gratefulness is both a feeling and a personality trait. Some folks are simply more prone to feeling appreciative on a regular basis.

Is It a Feeling?

Gratitude is both a fleeting emotion and a personality attribute. In all circumstances, gratitude entails first acknowledging that one has achieved a nice result and second that good result is due to an external source.

Gratitude begins with appreciating the positive things in life. A materialistic culture that promotes perpetual seeking and views commodities as the source of happiness isn't conducive to thankfulness. However, it is not an insurmountable obstacle to its development. Envy, cynicism, and narcissism, in particular, are all thieves of thankfulness. Indeed, cultivating appreciation may be at least a partial antidote to narcissism.

How Can You Practice Gratitude?

Simply being in the company of family and friends can make you feel more appreciative. Being more appreciative of life and feeling less pessimistic also encourages you to be more grateful. When faced with a difficult decision, seeing it as a gift can be helpful; in fact, some people like having to make such a decision.

What Makes YOU Grateful?

This varies from person to person, and we all have different levels of desire to experience and show thankfulness. It could be something as simple as a refreshing spring shower, simply because rain cleans everything. People feel good about themselves when they participate in a more specific deed, such as volunteering to aid others.

Rachel was grateful for so many things in her journey. She was (and is) grateful for knowing what it was like to have very little and full of gratitude for being able to provide for her family in all the ways she could.

She was grateful that her kids appreciated what they have, and now, as adults, they work hard to maintain it. They carry on the same legacy that she had started. She showed them how to take care of others and be grateful for everything that they have or sometimes don't have.

She is grateful for the time she was away from Cantor and working with a woman named Jen. This was a woman who could understand what Rachel was feeling and going through - as a mom and as a woman doing the same job. They both knew the feeling of being stretched as thin as one could be. Like Rachel, she was a super mom and an amazing broker. The time they spent together working side by side was a real blessing, and Rachel saw from Jen and her family what ultimate kindness and compassion look like. It was where Rachel needed to be while she healed.

She often thinks back at the phone call she received from her boss, Danny, asking her to come back home to work at BGC after she had left Cantor for a while. She was hesitant because they really hadn't spoken after she left, except on one day a year. Every 9/11, Rachel would wish Danny and the firm good luck raising money for many amazing charities. It was a piece that was missing, but she was glad somebody equally trustworthy was working at the helm for the cause. She knew in her heart that she should be raising money in the name of all the amazing people who had lost their lives and whom she loved so dearly; she wanted to do that. So, she went back. She was thrilled when she returned, and she felt she was where she should be.

Today, she is still working there, and although the stories may be told less frequently, she and Cappy will throw out a one-liner from one of the boys, and the stories will start to be told again. She is with the people who will never forget about who was there and what happened on 9/11.

Their memories and legacy will stay alive in those rooms for many years to come. Some of their children are there working and carrying it on. The amazing friendships that were built still tell the stories of before their friends were lost.

Chapter 8 – Legacy of Others Left Behind

Rachel is one of the so many people left behind on 9/11, feeling the loss of a loved one, family member, or very close friend. Such a cruel and senseless act of violence brought into the world that day left so many without the chance to say goodbye. These are a few stories and memories of others left behind.

***

I still talk to my dad, Timothy Grazioso, every day. And he talks right back to me. Maybe not with words, but I feel his love in a way that could not be more real. We have discussed many things in the time since he has gone.

Mostly we review the lessons and values he instilled into me and my twin sister, Lauren, and how they guide us today. The most important of these were family values, which he prioritized above all else. It was the mantra by which he lived his meaningful, albeit short, life, and we honor him today by living ours the same.

I remember how he used to tickle us to wake up each weekend as he unselfishly commuted to Florida, where we lived. We moved there as he thought the climate would be better for Lauren, who has Type 1 Diabetes. During the week, he lived alone in a Brooklyn apartment where he kept a complete set of our schoolbooks to do homework with us over the phone. But when Friday came and we were together, those weekends were really special.

After the tickle wake-up call, he would carry us downstairs and make us breakfast. His French toast was second to none. As tired as he was after working all week and traveling home, he would sleep on the floor between mine and Lauren's rooms in case we got scared during the night.

He would always cook us chicken piccata for dinner on Sunday nights before returning to New York for the next work week, where he was Cantor Fitzgerald's Chief Operating Officer of OTC Trading. As busy as he was, he always made time to write us a handwritten note under our pillow saying how much fun he had that weekend and how much he loved and missed us already.

He continues to tell me how proud he is of me and how he knew I could do it even when I had doubts. He provides me with guidance and confidence as I'm humbled to be working for the place that, for ten years, he helped build and gratefully contributed his all to its growth and success.

I feel my best when I reflect on the day's events and know I conducted myself and made decisions based on how I believe would have made him proud. Our mother saved a pair of my father's shoes for my sister and me to keep. She told us to marry someone who could fill even half of them, as those shoes were filled with love, compassion, work ethic, and kindness.

I'm so proud to be one of "Timmy's girls." My dad ascribed to the adage that "everything happens for a reason." While after 20 years, I am still searching for the reason that we lost him so early in our lives. His perseverance, determination, and unconditional love taught me to never give up, and his stubbornness taught me to refuse to accept that I may never find it.

Briana Grazioso

***

I was only six years old when my father was killed on September 11, 2001. I do not have memories of the time we spent together. It is difficult for me to think about him without getting emotional. Despite that, he is constantly on my mind. While I enjoy hearing stories about him from my family and his friends when the opportunity arises, I still cannot help but wonder what my life would have been like had he not died. I imagine it would be completely different because much of what I have undertaken has been a direct result of 9/11.

Whenever I find myself in a tough spot, I think of whether what I'm doing would be something that he would be proud of. I am not trying to become my father. I am trying to carry myself in a manner that he would be proud of. It is impossible to take the stories I've heard about him and be able to understand who he was. I just try to take what I've learned about him to help guide me as I grow.

Michael McHugh, 26

***

It's strange because I feel like all of my real memories are from post-9/11 life. I never got the chance to really know my father, and that is why I love hearing stories from so many people who did get the chance to know him. My father was a bigger guy and quite the athlete, and as someone who was able to play college lacrosse, my favorite thing to hear from my family and other people was how similar we are in how we carry ourselves on the field.

Every time I stepped on the field at Lehigh, where I went to school, I would think about making him proud, and I hope I was able to accomplish that. September 11th is obviously a tough day for myself and my family, but I would be lying if I said it wasn't something I look forward to every year. I receive upward of 50 texts from so many different people letting me know that they are there for me whenever I need it, and I think that speaks volumes about the person my father was.

I look forward to it because it is one of the few days that people really come together and show support for one another. There is a community of people whose lives were majorly affected by the attacks, and when I meet one of them, we immediately connect on another level.

The 9/11 attacks proved Americans could be there for one another when it matters most.

Christian McHugh, 23

***

My dad has been instrumental in my growth as a person, particularly in the past few years, as I've come to understand and appreciate the type of person he was and who he would want me to be. I strive to make every decision with him in mind in pursuit of making him proud.

He taught me to seize the moment, accept the things that I cannot change, and change the things that are in my control, all without saying anything. I might not have spent a lot of time with him, but I know my dad because he lives within my brothers and me. We share the stoicism, humor, athleticism, and character that define who he was as a person, and I'm grateful for the opportunity to continue and strengthen his legacy.

Connor McHugh, 21

***

My father, Tim Soulas, worked next to Rachel Hatton at Cantor Fitzgerald for many years before he was killed on 9/11. While I was only in second grade at the time, I have been lucky to be supported by the network my father built since his passing. From aunts and uncles living at my house to help my pregnant mother support her five kids immediately after 9/11 to coaches and mentors guiding me through my academic and professional career, someone has always been there to have my back.

Every 9/11 anniversary, Rachel would visit my family at the Tower of Remembrance in the Shrine of Saint Joseph to pay her respects. I was fortunate enough to get a job at Cantor Fitzgerald (now BGC) after I graduated college in 2016 and worked with the same people as my father did. I thought I'd heard every story about my father as a kid, but every week there seems to be a new memory shared with me.

One of my favorites is my dad nearly killing his client at the driving range with such a terrible golf swing – something I have in common with him. When I first started at BGC, I was joking around with some of the guys on Rachel's desk before she stopped me and said, *"Oh my God, that's exactly something that Tim would've said!"* It's a very cool feeling to hear I have the same type of humor as my dad. After all, I was only seven years old when he passed.

Working at BGC for five years now has been an incredible journey, and the people who worked with my dad have helped to shape my career. I started writing tickets, then moved to broker trades, and even had a brief stint abroad in Hong Kong before the pandemic cut that chapter of my life a little short. I would never have thought I'd be in the position I am today without their help, and I hope to continue carrying on his legacy as best as possible.

Chris Soulas

***

Dear Todd,

I can't believe it's been 20 years. Twenty years since a normal cloudless September day changed everything. It changed all of us; it changed me. Not a day goes by that I don't think of you … that I don't miss you. Every time I go to Yankee Stadium, eat chicken parmesan, listen to U2, or see a black BMW (thanks to Rachel), I think of you. And every time I see a dark-haired, short, 25-year-old confident, fearless, cocky dude with the biggest smile on the planet, I miss you. (Sorry for the short comment, but you know it's true!)

I miss the brother you were, and I miss the brother that you would have been. My two sons would have loved you (and you them)! Chris shares your live-every-day-to-its-fullest mentality and Nicky your unwavering confidence and cheeky smile.

As you know, like Rachel, I am also one of those left behind. Two brothers. Same profession. Same company. One in New York that day, one in London. Not only did I lose you. But, like Rachel, I also lost all of you. Pepe, Chris, Timmy, Tim, Keith, Andy, Teddy, Phil, Rob. The list goes on.

I miss them all. I try to honor all of you every day by being the best friend, dad, husband, uncle, and person I can be. I also give thanks to the one bright spot from that horrendous day. That dad got out of the building.

Heather and I have a mantra from a poem written by Anya Garcia, an American Airlines flight attendant who lost her entire crew on AAL flight 11 that day; Make it Count. For you, for them, for everyone who lost their lives that day, we try to make every day and everything we do count.

Here's a passage from the poem.

'Because of them, I'm a nicer, better person. Because of them, I reach ever more deeply in my heart to find compassion for the angry, the frustrated, the lonely, for people just like you and me. For it seems to me that if they had the gift of time on this imperfect earth, they too would reach for the ultimate power of human connection. Their mantra sustains me as I breathe in each moment, once for my precious life, twice for all of them.'

"Make it Count."

Love,

Jordan

Made in the USA
Columbia, SC
13 November 2021